Church Year

Series B
Lent • Easter • Ascension • Pentecost

Study Guide

By Mark Brighton

CPH
SAINT LOUIS

Edited by Thomas J. Doyle

Write to the Library for the Blind, 1333 S. Kirkwood Road, St. Louis, MO 63122-7295 to obtain this study in braille or in large print for the visually impaired.

1   2   3   4   5   6   7   8   9   10   05   04   03   02   01   00   99   98   97   96

Contents

Introduction

About the Series

This course is 1 of 12 in the Church Year series. The Bible studies in this series are tied to the 3-year lectionary. These studies give participants the opportunity to explore the Old Testament lesson (or lesson from the book of Acts during the Easter season), the Epistle lesson, and the Gospel lesson appointed for each Sunday of the church year. Also, optional studies give participants the opportunity to study in-depth the lessons appointed for festival days that fall on days other than Sunday (e.g., Ascension Day, Reformation, Christmas, Christmas Eve, Maundy Thursday, Good Friday, Epiphany).

Book 1 for years A, B, and C in the lectionary series will include 17 studies for the Scripture lessons appointed for the Sundays and festival days in Advent, Christmas, and Epiphany. Book 2 will include 17 studies for the lessons appointed for the Sundays and festival days in Lent and Easter and of lessons appointed for Ascension and Pentecost. Book 3 (15 sessions) and 4 (15 sessions) for years A, B, and C will include studies that focus on the lessons appointed for the Pentecost season.

After a brief review and textual study of the Scripture lessons appointed for a Sunday or festival day, each study is designed to help participants draw conclusions about each of the lessons, compare the lessons, discover a unifying theme in the lessons (if possible), and apply the theme to their lives. At the end of each study, the Scripture lessons for the next Sunday and/or festival day are assigned for participants to read in preparation for the next study. The Leaders Guide for each course provides additional information on appointed lessons, answers to the questions in the Study Guide, a suggested process for teaching the study, and devotional or worship activities tied to the theme.

May the Holy Spirit richly bless you as you study God's Word!

Session 1

First Sunday in Lent

Genesis 22:1–18; Romans 8:31–39; Mark 1:12–15

<hr>

Focus

Theme: *Obedience and Endurance from Grace*

Law/Gospel Focus

God requires His people to be obedient to His will even as they face temptation and hardship. In Christ, God graciously forgives the disobedience of His children, puts away their guilt, and assures them of eternal life in heaven.

Objectives

By the grace of God in Christ we will
1. understand more clearly the nature of testing and temptation;
2. see how the love of God in Christ creates obedience and endurance in the lives of God's people;
3. give thanks for the forgiveness and salvation God gives in Christ;
4. remind ourselves daily of what Christ has done for us so that the Holy Spirit might strengthen our obedience and endurance.

Opening Worship

Leader: In the name of the Father and of the Son and of the Holy Spirit.
Participants: Amen!
Leader: Fear not, for I have redeemed you;
Participants: I have summoned you by name; you are Mine.
Leader: When you pass through the waters,
Participants: I will be with you;
Leader: And when you pass through the rivers,

Participants: They will not sweep over you.
Leader: When you walk through the fire,
Participants: You will not be burned; the flames will not set you ablaze.
Leader: For I am the LORD, your God,
Participants: The Holy One of Israel, your Savior.
(Isaiah 43:1–3)

Introduction

People commonly think that Lent is a rather dreary time of the church year. In fact, Mardi Gras originated from people's desire to have as much fun as possible before Ash Wednesday and the Lenten season compelled people to fast, pray, and think about their own sinfulness. People thought they could have no fun until Lent was over.

While it is true that Lent begins as a period of repentance and fasting, the lessons throughout the season cast a different light on the meaning of the season. What is important about Lent is not the fasting or prayer or other activities which people think will enhance their relationship with God. Instead, the important focus of Lent is on what Christ did to restore people's relationship to God.

The lessons for this week, for example, emphasize the importance of obedience to God's will in the face of testing and temptation. But what God *does* when we are tempted is far more important than what we *do* when we are tempted. Far more important than our obedience to God's will is Christ's obedience. And far more important than our sinful failings is God's forgiveness.

1. What are some common temptations that people face?

2. How can God's people combat these temptations?

3. What sorts of things do people experience that cause them at times to question God's love?

Inform

Look at the brief summaries of the Scripture lessons for the First Sunday in Lent. Then answer the questions.

Genesis 22:1–18—Abraham and Sarah finally had a son. He filled their lives with joy. But a few years later, God commanded Abraham to sacrifice Isaac. Despite the inner turmoil which he no doubt felt, through faith Abraham was able to trust God's graciousness. In this way he not only found the will to obey God, but he also received God's blessing.

Romans 8:31–39—The apostle Paul writes a crescendo of God's love and grace in Christ. In the face of their own sinful failings and suffering, God's people can be absolutely certain that because of Christ God always loves them and will never leave or forsake them.

Mark 1:12–15—Before He began His public ministry, Jesus was tempted by Satan for 40 days in the wilderness. Jesus never yielded to temptation. He thus not only demonstrated that He is without sin, but also that He understands the nature of temptation and can give His people victory when they are tempted.

1. Remember that Isaac's name literally meant "laughter." How might this name describe the effect that Isaac had on Abraham's and Sarah's lives? How does this name help us understand the turmoil Abraham must have experienced when God commanded him to sacrifice Isaac?

2. Abraham may have also had difficulty understanding why God would give this command. Look at Genesis 21:12. How does this verse help us understand the questions Abraham may have had when God told him to sacrifice Isaac? Now look at Genesis 22:5. What did Abraham tell his servants? What do these words tell us about Abraham's expectations of God concerning Isaac? For help, look at Hebrews 11:17–19.

3. In the Epistle lesson Paul touches upon two reasons that people doubt God's love. What is the reason implied in verses 33 and 34? What is the reason implied in verse 35? How does God answer both these threats (37–39)?

4. Jesus was tempted by Satan for 40 days in the wilderness. The words *forty* and *wilderness* would be very familiar to Mark's readers who knew their Scripture. What incident would come to mind? How did the people of God fare during that time of testing? By contrast, how did Jesus fare during His time of testing?

5. How did Satan tempt Jesus? Matthew 4:1–11 and Luke 4:1–13 provide some explicit answers, but look also at Hebrews 4:15–16. What other temptations would you suppose Jesus faced throughout the days of His earthly ministry? What encouragement does the author of Hebrews derive from the fact that Jesus was tempted in every way that we are?

Connect

1. What sorts of things do parents require their children to do? Does a parent's love depend on the child's obedience? Should it? Why or why not?

2. Paul indicated that suffering and hardship threaten to separate people from the love of God. What helped Abraham endure the turmoil he must have felt as he and Isaac walked those last steps to the mountain? See Romans 8:37–39.

3. What comfort does God provide for His people when they face various hardships, calamities, diseases, and death? Look at 2 Corinthians 4:16–18. How do these words provide comfort to a believer who faces and endures hardship?

4. Paul also indicated that guilt threatens to separate people from God's love. How do people act when they feel guilty about something they have done to somebody? Do these activities help or hurt a relationship? How does guilt hurt a relationship with God?

5. What does God say in Christ about our guilt? Look at Romans 8:1–2. What comfort do these verses bring when a person falls repeatedly, even into the same sin?

Vision

To Do This Week

1. Find two 3 × 5 cards or small pieces of paper. On one write the words of Romans 8:1 for meditation and prayer when you are tempted and fall into sin. On the other write the words of

2 Corinthians 4:17 for meditation and prayer when you encounter hardship and suffering. Carry the cards with you.
2. Make a list of things you would like to do this week to demonstrate your love for Christ.
3. Look for ways to share God's forgiveness and love with another person who you know is laboring with guilt or suffering.

Closing Worship

Sing stanza 1 of "My Faith Looks Up to Thee."
My faith looks up to Thee,
Thou Lamb of Calvary,
Savior divine.
Now, hear me while I pray;
Take all my guilt away;
Oh, let me from this day
Be wholly Thine!

Scripture Lessons for Next Sunday

In preparation for the next session, read Genesis 28:10–17 (18–22), Romans 5:1–11, and Mark 8:31–38.

Session 2

Second Sunday in Lent

Genesis 28:10–17 (18–22); Romans 5:1–11; Mark 8:31–38

Focus

Theme: *The Great Exchange*

Law/Gospel Focus

Because of sin, people squander, destroy, or lose what they hold dear. Yet in Christ's death on the cross, God restores eternal riches to those who trust in His mercy and grace.

Objectives

By the grace of God in Christ we will
1. understand more clearly the exchange of fortunes between Christ and sinful people;
2. learn more about what it means to carry a cross;
3. place our hope on eternal, heavenly treasures;
4. help someone who is lost.

Opening Worship

Leader: In the name of the Father and of the Son and of the Holy Spirit.

Participants: Amen!

Leader: The LORD is my shepherd, I shall not be in want.

Participants: He makes me lie down in green pastures,

Leader: He leads me beside quiet waters,

Participants: He restores my soul.

Leader: He guides me in paths of righteousness for His name's sake.

Participants: Even though I walk through the valley of the shadow of death,

Leader: I will fear no evil, for You are with me;

Participants: Your rod and Your staff, they comfort me.

Leader: You prepare a table before me in the presence of my enemies.
Participants: You anoint my head with oil; my cup overflows.
Leader: Surely goodness and love will follow me all the days of my life,
Participants: And I will dwell in the house of the LORD forever. (Psalm 23)

Introduction

Most people in the United States will move several times. Young people leave home to go away to a college or university, the elderly sometimes move to retirement communities, and those in between may move several times for a variety of reasons.

1. When was the last time you moved? Why did you move?

2. What did you lose when you moved? What did you gain?

In the Old Testament lesson for this Sunday we see how God is gracious to His people when they lose belongings, loved ones, and are in danger of losing life. The Epistle and Gospel lessons affirm that God in fact brings new life to those who have lost all things.

Inform

Look at the brief summaries of the Scripture lessons for the Second Sunday in Lent. Then answer the questions.

Genesis 28:10–17 (18–22)—Jacob, with help from his mother, Rebekah, had just tricked Isaac so that he would receive his father's blessing. Esau, Jacob's brother, was bitter and entertained thoughts of killing Jacob. So Jacob fled to Haran, where his uncle Laban lived. While he was on the way, the Lord spoke to Jacob in a dream, promising to be with him and bless him.

Romans 5:1–11—Paul here gives many reasons how and why the people of God have peace and joy through Jesus Christ. They have hope in the glory of God, they rejoice in suffering, and they can be confident of God's favor in Christ.

Mark 8:31–38—After Peter confessed that Jesus was the Messiah, Jesus began to teach the disciples plainly about His coming suffering, death, and resurrection. Peter objected to what Jesus was saying, but after harshly rebuking Peter, Jesus further explained how death on a cross was an integral part of salvation.

1. Remember that Jacob had just left home for the first time. Furthermore, he was not leaving on the best of terms with his brother, Esau. As Jacob settled down for the night, what sorts of things might he have been thinking about his family? His welfare and safety? His future?

2. What things did the Lord promise Jacob in the dream? Why would these promises be especially meaningful to Jacob?

3. Paul states that when God's people suffer, they can still rejoice. What reasons does Paul give for this statement?

4. In Romans 5:6–11, and especially verse 10, what contrast does Paul make? How does this contrast affect the confidence of God's people?

5. Why did Peter rebuke Jesus when He began to speak about His suffering and death? What do you suppose Peter thought should happen to Jesus? How do you think Peter responded to Jesus' rebuke?

15

6. Why did Jesus respond to Peter by saying, "Get behind Me, Satan!" For help, compare Peter's rebuke of Jesus with Satan's temptation of Jesus in the wilderness (Matthew 4:1–11).

7. Jesus not only talked about His own suffering and death, but also insisted that His followers must "deny" themselves and take up their "cross." What do you suppose He meant? What is implied in verses 35–36 and verse 38?

Connect

1. What is a "cross" that believers carry? For help, look at the following passages and discuss examples for each.

   Matthew 5:11–12

   Matthew 10:37–39

   Romans 8:13–14

2. As you think of the what it means to carry a "cross" for Christ, what comfort does God bring when you consider the way He treated Jacob? How does God bring His own eternal blessings for each of the areas of sacrifice listed in the previous question?

3. Because God loves sinful people, He sent Christ to make a gracious exchange with them. Read 2 Corinthians 8:9. What did Christ take from us? What did Christ give to us?

4. Place yourself in the following situation. You are a prisoner in Auschwitz in the Second World War. Last night two people from your barracks attempted to escape, but they were caught and killed. Moreover, to make an example that all such behavior would be punished severely, the next day the guards selected five additional people in your group, whom they intended to lock in a room and starve to death. You were chosen. But as you were about to be led away, an older prisoner, whom you had come to know as a kind and giving person, stepped forward next to you and said to the guards, "I would like you to take me instead. I am old, this person is young and has a family." The guard agreed. Eight days later you learned that the older prisoner had finally died, the last of the five.

Write a letter to a loved one, explaining what happened. Then consider volunteering to read your letter to the group.

Vision

To Do This Week

1. This week during your devotions, make a list of the sacrifices that you must make as a follower of Christ. For each item, pray for forgiveness and/or strength where appropriate. Remembering that Christ comes to make a gracious exchange with His people, what promise from God can you list beside each sacrifice?

2. Help a person this week who like Jacob may be lonely because they have lost loved ones, or are worried about their welfare.

Closing Worship

Sing stanza 2 of "My Faith Looks Up to Thee."
> May Thy rich grace impart
> Strength to my fainting heart,
> My zeal inspire!
> As Thou hast died for me,
> Oh, may my love to Thee
> Pure, warm, and changeless be,
> A living fire!

Scripture Lessons for Next Sunday

In preparation for the next session, read Exodus 20:1–17, 1 Corinthians 1:22–25, and John 2:13–22.

Session 3

Third Sunday in Lent

Exodus 20:1–17; 1 Corinthians 1:22–25; John 2:13–22

Focus

Theme: *The Heart of the Matter*

Law/Gospel Focus

God makes His will known in the Ten Commandments, which people cannot keep perfectly because of sin. In Christ, God forgives their disobedience and graciously blesses even imperfect acts of obedience done in faith.

Objectives

By the grace of God in Christ we will
1. understand more fully the claims of God's commandments and the nature of sinful disobedience;
2. learn how faith in Christ is at the heart of true obedience;
3. remind ourselves daily of God's forgiveness in Christ, and how we can show our love for God and others by keeping the Commandments.

Opening Worship

Leader: In the name of the Father and of the Son and of the Holy Spirit.
Participants: Amen!
Leader: Create in me a pure heart, O God,
Participants: And renew a steadfast spirit within me.
Leader: O Lord, open my lips,
Participants: And my mouth will declare Your praise.
Leader: You do not delight in sacrifice, or I would bring it;
Participants: You do not take pleasure in burnt offerings.
Leader: The sacrifices of God are a broken spirit;
Participants: A broken and contrite heart, O God, You will not despise.

Introduction

Imagine that you are the parent of a 3-year-old child and one day the child disappears into a room for 20 minutes. All is quiet, too quiet in fact! You are just about to rise out of your chair and see if everything is okay when your child finally emerges from the room with a painting. On the paper you see streaks of blues, greens, and yellows. Your child has obviously been hard at work on the picture, which, you are told, is a whale. How would you react if the child presented the picture to you and said:

a. "I made this for you. Do you love me?"

b. "I made this for you. Can I now have a piece of candy?"

c. "I made this for you. I love you."

Which would you rather have your child say? Why?

The Old Testament lesson for this week records the Ten Commandments. In this lesson we will then consider the nature of obedience to God.

Inform

Look at the brief summaries of the Scripture lessons for the Third Sunday in Lent. Then answer the questions.

Exodus 20:1–17—Through many mighty acts and miracles, God had delivered His people from slavery in Egypt and provided for all their needs as they traveled in the wilderness. When they arrived at Mount Sinai, they set up camp, and Moses ascended the mountain to receive from the Lord instructions which he would then pass on to the people. Beginning with the Ten Commandments, the Lord established a covenant with Israel.

1 Corinthians 1:22–25—Here Paul explains that God does not work

as people expect. The cross is an offense to some and foolishness to others. But it is how God brings salvation to sinful people.

John 2:13–22—On entering the temple, Jesus found the temple courts had been turned into a marketplace by people who were selling animals for sacrifice and exchanging foreign currency for temple currency. After Jesus drove them out, the Jewish leaders asked what miracle Jesus would perform to prove His authority before God. Jesus referred to His resurrection as this sign.

1. Exodus 20:1–17 begins to define a covenant relationship which God desired to have with His people. (See the *Concordia Self-Study Bible* text note for 20:2.) Who initiated this covenant? What had the Lord done for his people? How were the people to respond to the Lord? What motivated their response?

2. How are the Ten Commandments reflected in the two commandments which sum up the entire law, " 'Love the Lord your God with all your heart and with all your soul and with all your strength and with all your mind;' and, 'Love your neighbor as yourself' " (Luke 10:27)?

3. Remember that the Ten Commandments condemn sins of commission (wrong behavior) and omission (the absence of right behavior). Remember, too, that this includes sins of thought, word, and deed. Provide some examples both of the forbidden behavior and the required behavior for the Commandments listed below.

Have no other Gods.

Do not take the name of the Lord in vain.

Remember the Sabbath day.

Honor father and mother.

Do not murder.

Do not steal.

Do not commit adultery.

Do not give false testimony.

Do not covet.

4. Referring to the Epistle lesson, what miraculous signs do you suppose Jews wanted from Jesus, but did not find? Why would they find the cross of Christ such a stumbling block?

5. Why is human wisdom "foolish" before God? For help, refer to 1 Corinthians 1:21 and 2:14.

6. Referring to the Gospel lesson, pilgrims who came to the temple would have to purchase animals for sacrifice. Therefore the sellers and money changers might have thought they were helping people by providing for the pilgrim's needs. Why do you suppose their activity received such harsh condemnation from Jesus?

7. Many people throughout history have claimed to have come from God and to speak for God. Why is the resurrection of Christ such a conclusive sign of His uniquely divine authority?

Connect

1. Doctors commonly take X-rays of the body in an effort to reach a proper diagnosis about their patients. The Commandments have been called "X-rays of the soul." What diagnosis do they provide about people and their relationship to God? For help see Romans 3:20 and Romans 7:7. Can people ever earn God's approval by keeping the Commandments?

2. Paul in Galatians wrote, "The Law was put in charge to lead us to Christ" (3:24). What do you suppose he meant? What does God provide in Christ that people cannot find by keeping the Law? For help, refer to Romans 8:1–4.

3. The author of Hebrews states, "Without faith it is impossible to please God" (Hebrews 11:6). Recall the opening illustration about the child who painted a picture.
   a. Many people try to keep the Ten Commandments because they fear that if they don't, God will not love them (corresponding to statement *a* in the illustration). Do you suppose such obedience pleases God? Why or why not?

   b. Others try to make themselves worthy of God's blessings by keeping the Commandments (corresponding to statement *b*). Do you suppose such obedience pleases God? Why or why not?

c. When a parent receives a picture from a child who loves and trusts the parent and simply wants to make the parent happy (corresponding to statement *c* in the illustration), what does the parent do with such a picture even though it is not perfect? Why? How does this correspond to how God views the obedience of believers?

4. What is at the heart of obedience? For help, refer to 1 John 4:19.

Vision

To Do This Week

1. Take time during family or personal devotions to explore further one or more of the Ten Commandments. Remember that as the Commandments expose our failures before God and others, Christ forgives us.
2. Looking at the Ten Commandments again, what might you do to demonstrate your love for God and others?

Closing Worship

Sing stanza 1 of "May We Your Precepts, Lord, Fulfill."
> May we Your precepts, Lord, fulfill
> And do on earth our Father's will
> As angels do above;
> Still walk in Christ, the living way,
> With all Your children and obey
> The law of Christian love.

Scripture Lessons for Next Sunday

In preparation for the next session, read Numbers 21:4–9, Ephesians 2:4–10, and John 3:14–21.

Session 4

Fourth Sunday in Lent

Numbers 21:4–9; Ephesians 2:4–10; John 3:14–21

Focus

Theme: *A Gracious Disposition*

Law/Gospel Focus

Be thankful for all of God's blessings and trust in His grace. For God freely gives all heavenly blessings in Christ.

Objectives

By the grace of God in Christ we will
1. understand better why we complain before God;
2. repent of sinful complaints;
3. rejoice in God's grace in Christ;
4. describe ways to handle legitimate complaints;
5. give thanks for God's blessings.

Opening Worship

Leader: In the name of the Father and of the Son and of the Holy Spirit.
Participants: Amen!
Leader:　　Give thanks to the LORD, for He is good;
Participants: His love endures forever.
Leader:　　Let the redeemed of the LORD say this—
Participants: Those He redeemed from the hand of the foe,
Leader:　　Those He gathered from the lands,
Participants: From east and west, from north and south.
Leader:　　Let them give thanks to the LORD for His unfailing love
Participants: And His wonderful deeds for men,
Leader:　　For He satisfies the thirsty
Participants: And fills the hungry with good things.
　　　　　(Psalm 107:1–3, 8–9)

Introduction

Imagine that while the family was out for the day, you decided to clean the entire house and wash the dirty clothes. After working most of the day with little time to sit, you then made dinner for the family. But when they came home, they failed to notice how clean the house was. Furthermore, when you sat down for dinner, one of the children complained, "Why do we have to eat this? I don't like it."

a. How would you feel? Why?

b. What would you like to do or say to the person who complained at the dinner table?

c. Why do you suppose people complain?

The Bible calls on the people of God to give thanks to the Lord. However, God's children often spend much time complaining, and as a consequence, not only are they unhappy, but they also hurt and frustrate others. More seriously, their complaints indicate their lack of trust in God's love and grace. The lessons for today will help us understand better the nature of complaints and how God responds to our needs.

Inform

Look at the brief summaries of the Scripture lessons for the Fourth Sunday in Lent. Then answer the questions.

Numbers 21:4–9—The Israelites had been in the wilderness for 40 years and were finally going back to the land of Canaan. They had to take a significant detour around the land of Edom and eventually lost patience, complaining again about the food they had to eat. God punished them by sending venomous snakes into their camp, but He also graciously provided healing by means of the bronze serpent.

Ephesians 2:4–10—Paul emphasizes our unity with Christ and how our salvation is a gift from God.

John 3:14–21—A Pharisee by the name of Nicodemus came one night to inquire of Jesus about salvation. In some of the most succinct Gospel statements to be found in all of Scripture, Jesus responded to

Nicodemus by affirming that God gives life through His only-begotten Son. Whoever has faith in Him has God's salvation.

1. In the Old Testament lesson, why do you suppose the Israelites complained so bitterly on this occasion? Remember that this was not the first time they had complained about the manna. See also Numbers 11:4ff.

2. Why did God react so harshly against their complaints?

3. Is there any significance to the manner in which God provided healing for the people?

4. In the Epistle lesson, Paul accents our unity with Christ. What three things do we receive from this unity? See especially verses 4–6. How do we become united with Christ? For help see Romans 6:3–4.

5. Paul mentions several attributes of God that are the cause of His saving activity in Christ. What are they? What are their significance for us?

6. In the Gospel lesson Jesus compares what will happen to Him to what God did by means of the serpent mentioned in the Old Testament lesson. What points of comparison are there between Christ and the bronze serpent?

7. How does God bring salvation through His only-begotten Son? Why was it necessary that God give His Son? For help see Romans 3:22–24.

8. Jesus went on to explain how God judges people. What is the criteria for judgment? When does this judgment take place?

Connect

1. List some reasons why people complain.
   a. About themselves

   b. About their jobs

   c. About their homes

   d. About churches

   e. About God

2. It has been observed that a drowning man will not complain about the size of the boat that comes to rescue him. Did the Israelites in the Old Testament have a legitimate complaint against God? How could the Israelites have acted differently?

3. Does God have a legitimate complaint against humankind? According to the Gospel, how does God voice His complaint?

4. Working through the above list, which complaints do you think are legitimate? Which are not? Instead of complaining, what might a person do differently? For help, look up the following passages:

Philippians 4:6–7

Psalm 103:1–5

Romans 12:14

Matthew 5:44

Matthew 18:15

Colossians 3:13

Vision

To Do This Week

1. On 3 × 5 cards, write the complaints you have. Put one on each card. During the week, pray about each of the cards you make. At the end of the week, determine what you might do in each area instead of complaining. Write your ideas on the back of the cards.

2. Use question 1 in "Connect" to list how God has blessed you in each area. During your devotions, give thanks for these blessings.

Closing Worship

Sing stanza 1 of "Christ, the Life of All the Living"
> Christ, the life of all the living,
> Christ, the death of death, our foe,
> Christ, Yourself for me once giving
> To the darkest depths of woe;
> Through Your suff'ring, death, and merit
> Life eternal I inherit,
> Thousand, thousand thanks are due,
> Dearest Jesus, unto You.

Scripture Lessons for Next Sunday

In preparation for the next session, read Jeremiah 31:31–34, Hebrews 5:7–9, and John 12:20–33.

Session 5

Fifth Sunday in Lent

Jeremiah 31:31–34; Hebrews 5:7–9; John 12:20–33

Focus

Theme: *The Deal of a Lifetime*

Law/Gospel Focus

If people attempt to enter into a relationship with God, they are obligated to uphold God's stipulations as summarized in the Law. Yet people cannot uphold God's law. God responds by entering into a relationship with sinful people through His Son, Jesus Christ.

Objectives

By the grace of God in Christ we will
1. explore what it means to be in a covenant relationship with God;
2. compare and contrast the biblical concepts of "Old Covenant" with "New Covenant;"
3. give thanks that God by His grace initiated and carried out the work of establishing and making good His promise to save and to bless His people.

Opening Worship

Leader: In the name of the Father and of the Son and of the Holy Spirit.
Participants: Amen!
Leader: Create in me a pure heart, O God,
Participants: And renew a steadfast spirit within me.
Leader: Do not cast me from Your presence
Participants: Or take Your Holy Spirit from me.
Leader: Restore to me the joy of Your salvation
Participants: And grant me a willing spirit, to sustain me.
Leader: Then I will teach transgressors Your ways,

Introduction

People often make contractual agreements with each other. When a new car is sold, the auto dealer will enter into an agreement with the buyer to fix whatever breaks on the car for a fixed period of time. The same is true when people buy major appliances. Some contracts are simple, others are complex. When people buy homes, they sign a multitude of legal documents that detail the price of the home and the terms of the sale. Other contractual relationships are life changing. When people marry, they get a marriage license from a local court official. This document stipulates that two people have now entered into a marriage relationship.

1. List some of the contractual agreements you have entered into?

2. Why do people make contracts with each other?

3. Are there any consequences if a contract is broken?

Two weeks ago, on the Third Sunday in Lent, we saw how God made a covenant with the Israelites at Mount Sinai. A covenant is an ancient contractual arrangement between two parties. As with modern contracts, an ancient covenant would contain stipulations and would be considered binding. The Old Testament tells us that God wishes to make a new covenant with His people. Exactly how and why He does this is further explained in the Epistle and Gospel lessons appointed for this day.

Inform

Look at the brief summaries of the Scripture lessons for the Fifth Sunday in Lent. Then answer the questions.

Jeremiah 31:31–34—The Lord is going to make a new covenant with His people because they had broken His first covenant. This new covenant will be characterized by the forgiveness of God and the faithfulness of His people.

Hebrews 5:7–9—Among humankind Jesus alone walked in true obedience to the stipulations of the Old Covenant. Because He is the Son of God, His obedience became the cause and source of the New Covenant.

John 12:20–33—Some Greeks come to see Jesus. Jesus in response states that through His death all people may enter into a new covenant relationship with God.

1. When was the first covenant established, and of what did it consist? What had the Lord agreed to do? What were the Israelites obligated to do? For help look up Exodus 19:3–6, 24:3–8, and Deuteronomy 7:12–15, 6:4–9. Why did God enter into a covenant relationship with the Israelites? See Deuteronomy 7:7–8.

2. God states that the Israelites had broken this covenant. What incidents from the Old Testament can you think of to illustrate this? Why were the Israelites unable to keep the covenant?

3. What promises does the Lord make according to the New Covenant? See verses 33 and 34. Referring again to the passages

listed in question 1, what significant differences exist between the Old Covenant and the New Covenant?

4. How and when was the New Covenant ratified? For help, look at Hebrews 9:15.

5. In the Epistle lesson, the author states that Jesus "learned obedience from what He suffered." In view of the fact that Jesus was never disobedient (He is without sin), what do you suppose the author of Hebrews meant?

6. The author then states that Jesus, after His perfect obedience and suffering, became the source of salvation to all who believe. What connection is there between Christ's obedience and our salvation? For help see Romans 5:19. How might this help you understand what part Christ plays in the establishment of the New Covenant?

7. In the Gospel lesson, many Jews would not have thought that Greeks would be part of God's messianic kingdom. But how did Jesus react when He heard that Greeks had come to see Him?

8. What do you suppose Jesus meant in talking about a seed that falls to the ground and dies to produce more seeds? For help, refer also to verse 32.

9. When Jesus spoke here about His glory, He was ultimately thinking about what would happen through His death on the cross. In what sense can the cross be connected to His glory? For help, refer to your answer in question 8.

Connect

1. Is it possible to enter into a relationship with God based on the covenant stipulations God gave at Sinai? Why or why not? What are the consequences of breaking this covenant relationship?

2. Manufacturer warranties can be voided for a variety of reasons. What "warranty" does God establish for people in the New Covenant? Can anybody or anything declare this "warranty" null and void? See Romans 8:38–39 for help. Give an example of how the "warranty" God makes in Christ can bring a person hope and peace.

3. How does God in the New Covenant put His law "in our minds" and write it "on our hearts?" For help see John 14:6 and Hebrews 4:12.

4. In the Gospel we learn that God's covenant in Christ—the forgiveness of sins purchased and won by Christ for us on the cross— is meant for all people irrespective of who they are or even of what

they have done. Make a list of things your church does or might do to bring this good news to the people in your community. As you look at the list, how can you become involved?

Vision

To Do This Week

1. The disciples were involved in helping the Greeks see Jesus. This week think of one person who does not know Christ or believe in Him. What thing can you do or say this week that will introduce her/him to Jesus and His love? Pray for this person, and ask for God blessings upon your witness.
2. In your devotions, list those ways in which you have been unfaithful to God's will. Ask for God's forgiveness. Read John 3:16 and then at the bottom of the list write in red ink, "All these items are covered under the warranty of God's New Covenant in Christ."

Closing Worship

Sing stanzas 1 and 2 of "Jesus, Your Blood and Righteousness."

Jesus, Your blood and righteousness
My beauty are, my glorious dress;
Mid flaming worlds, in these arrayed,
With joy shall I lift up my head.

Bold shall I stand in that great day,
Cleansed and redeemed, no dept to pay;
For by Your cross absolved I am
From sin an guilt, from fear and shame.

Scripture Lessons for Next Sunday

In preparation for the next session, read Zechariah 9:9–10, Philippians 2:5–11, and Mark 15:1–39.

Session 6

Palm Sunday
(Sunday of the Passion)

Zechariah 9:9–10; Philippians 2:5–11; Mark 15:1–39

Focus

Theme: *The Humble King*

Law/Gospel Focus

Because of sin people rebel against God. They do not claim Him as their King and thus cannot dwell in His kingdom. But Christ came in humility to take away the curse of sin and reestablish the kingdom of God among us.

Objectives

By the grace of God in Christ we will
1. describe what it means to confess Christ is our King;
2. explain how the cross is an integral part of how Christ established His kingdom;
3. describe the blessings of living in God's kingdom.

Opening Worship

Leader: In the name of the Father and of the Son and of the Holy Spirit.
Participants: Amen!
Leader: Be merciful to me, O LORD, for I am in distress;
Participants: My eyes grow weak with sorrow, my soul and my body with grief.
Leader: My life is consumed by anguish
Participants: And my years by groaning;
Leader: My strength fails because of my affliction,
Participants: And my bones grow weak.
Leader: But I trust in You, O LORD;

Participants: I say, "You are my God."
Leader:　　　My times are in Your hands;
Participants: Deliver me from my enemies and from those who
　　　　　　　pursue me.
Leader:　　　Let Your face shine on Your servant;
Participants: Save me in Your unfailing love.
　　　　　　　(Psalm 31:9–10, 14–16)

Introduction

Today marks the beginning of Holy Week, when Christians around the world remember Christ's suffering and death. This week we as Christians will again sit in the upper room with Christ, reading in the gospels His final words and prayers for His disciples and receiving His body and blood in the bread and wine. We will go to Gethsemane and hear Christ's anguished prayers and witness the betrayal. We will be present at the trial before Caiaphas, where Christ is mocked and condemned. Then we will come before Pilate, see the king of the Jews sentenced to death, and journey to the cross.

Today is called the Sunday of the Passion because it focuses on these events, especially those of Good Friday. Today, however, is also known as Palm Sunday, so named because of the manner in which the Jews welcomed Jesus into Jerusalem. He came as the King of His people, yet He came humbly. In this lesson we will consider what kind of king Jesus is and how He establishes His kingdom among us.

1. How can a church extend the kingdom of Christ in the surrounding community?

2. How do people become part of Christ's kingdom?

Inform

Look at the brief summaries of the Scripture lessons for Palm Sunday (Sunday of the Passion). Then answer the questions.

Zechariah 9:9–10—Here the prophet calls God's covenant people to rejoice because a king will come to establish peace among all peoples.

Philippians 2:5–11—Paul from prison writes of Christ's humility and exaltation. Paul encourages the Christians at Philippi to have this same attitude amongst themselves.

Mark 15:1–39—Mark tells how Jesus the King stood trial before Pilate, who had Him whipped and crucified.

1. In the Old Testament lesson, what is so surprising about the manner in which the King will come to Israel? How ought a king be received among his people?

2. Matthew connects this passage to how Jesus came into Jerusalem. Read about it in Matthew 21:1–9. By doing this, what is Matthew telling us about Jesus? About how He entered Jerusalem?

3. Going back to Zechariah, what are the characteristic features of the kingdom that the coming King will establish?

4. The Epistle lesson can be divided into two parts, verses 6–8 and verses 9–11. The first half talks about Christ's humility, and the second half His glory. What two things mentioned in the first half illustrate Christ's humility? What is the characteristic feature of His glory? How are these verses connected? That is, how is Christ's humility connected to His glory?

5. Paul begins this entire section by encouraging the Philippians to have the same attitude as that of Christ. What do you suppose he meant? For help see Philippians 2:4. Remember also that Paul is writing these words from prison. How might the "attitude of Christ" have affected Paul's attitude? For help look also at Philippians 1:12–21.

6. Mark tells us the Jewish leaders brought Jesus before Pontius Pilate and accused Him of claiming to be King of the Jews. Was Jesus "guilty" of this charge? See Mark 15:2 and also Mark 14:61–62.

7. This charge amounted to treason, a crime punishable in the Roman Empire by death. Did Pilate appear at first to take this charge seriously? For help, see Mark 15:10 and John 19:4–6. What ultimately caused Pilate to hand Jesus over, even though he thought Jesus was innocent? See John 19:12 and Matthew 27:24.

8. Mark tells us only one thing that Jesus said on the cross. Why did Jesus say these words? For help, see Isaiah 53:10. What do these words tell us about Jesus' suffering on the cross? Did Jesus deserve to die? For help, see 2 Corinthians 5:21.

9. After Jesus' death, Mark tells us that in the curtain which divided the Holy Place from the Most Holy Place in the temple was torn in two. What is the significance of this event? For help, see Hebrews 9:8–12 and 10:19–20.

Connect

1. The Jews thought the Messiah would come and establish a glorious, powerful, earthly kingdom. When Jesus came as their king, they failed to recognize Him. Why? What are the characteristic features of the kingdom that Christ established on the cross? For help, see Romans 5:1–2 and Galatians 4:4–7.

2. People will sometimes evaluate the strength and vitality of a congregation by the number of its programs, the size of its membership, or the beauty of the facilities. How is Christ's kingdom established at a local congregation? What should be the characteristic features of the kingdom of Christ at a particular congregation? How does this knowledge help us more accurately assess the strength or programs of a congregation?

3. Paul's letter to the Philippians is known as his joyful letter, even though he wrote it from prison. Paul knew that Christ, who brings salvation through the cross, would save him. Recall a time when Christ brought comfort and help to you in the midst of suffering, hardship, or uncertainty. Write a paragraph describing your experience, and then share it with your group.

4. Mark tells us about the curtain in the temple to dramatically remind us that through Jesus we can come into the holy presence of God. List some ways by which people in your community can find access to the presence of God through Christ in your congregation.

Vision

To Do This Week

1. Remembering that Christ's kingdom is characterized by forgiveness and grace, make a list of how can you be instrumental in bringing others into His kingdom.
2. Read Psalm 22 and compare its contents to the passion narrative of Christ. Note especially that the Psalm ends with confidence. List how Christ gives you confidence in suffering, hardship, or uncertainty.

Closing Worship

Sing stanzas 1 and 3 of "Hosanna, Loud Hosanna."

Hosanna, loud hosanna, The little children sang;
Through pillared court and temple The lovely anthem rang.
To Jesus, who had blessed them, Close folded to His breast,
The children sang their praises, The simplest and the best.

"Hosanna in the highest!" That ancient song we sing,
For Christ is our Redeemer, The Lord of heav'n our King.
Oh, may we ever praise Him With heart and life and voice
And in His blissful presence Eternally rejoice!

Scripture Lessons for Maundy Thursday

In preparation for the next session, read Exodus 24:3–11, 1 Corinthians 10:16–17 (18–21), and Mark 14:12–26.

Session 7

Maundy Thursday

Exodus 24:3–11; 1 Corinthians 10:16–17 (18–21);
Mark 14:12–26

Focus

Theme: *A Heavenly Banquet*

Law/Gospel Focus

Fellowship with God and with each other is broken by sin.
Christ reestablishes this fellowship through His blood shed on
the cross.

Objectives

By the grace of God in Christ we will
1. realize how our fellowship with God and others is broken
   because of sin;
2. give thanks that God in Christ restores communion with
   Himself and others;
3. understand more clearly the background and meaning of
   the Lord's Supper;
4. give thanks that God will restore His people into His heavenly family.

Opening Worship

Leader: In the name of the Father and of the Son and of
the Holy Spirit.

Participants: Amen!

Leader: On this mountain the LORD Almighty will prepare
a feast of rich food for all peoples,

Participants: A banquet of aged wine—the best of meats and
the finest of wines.

Leader: On this mountain He will destroy the shroud that
enfolds all peoples,

Introduction

I can still smell the pot roast. It was just before noon on Sunday. Our family had gone to Sunday school and worship and now it was time for lunch. The moment I came into the kitchen, my mouth would begin to water as the deep aroma of gravy and rolls and roast beef filled the air. My sister and I would set the table with care. Then we would light the candles, sit down, and give thanks, and enjoy the meal.

1. Think for a moment of banquets or dinners that you have had with your family and friends. Describe one of these occasions to your group. Why does this occasion remain such a strong part of your memory?

2. Do families always experience strong bonds of love and attachment? Why or why not?

Today is known as Maundy Thursday, a day when Christians remember a banquet in the upper room that Christ shared with His disciples immediately before His arrest and crucifixion. It was on that occasion that Christ instituted the Sacrament of the Altar, passing the bread and wine and saying, "This is My body ... This is My blood."

He commanded His disciples to keep this celebration as a memorial of His death, and so tonight we also will receive the bread and the wine, and with it Christ's body and blood.

The Lord's Supper reminds us that in Christ we are united with God and with each other in one family. Not only that, Christ gives Himself in the meal to His people for the forgiveness of their sins. It is a time when we give thanks to God for His forgiveness and the assurance of our restoration to life with Him and all our loved ones in heaven. It is a heavenly banquet.

Inform

Look at the brief summaries of the Scripture lessons for Maundy Thursday. Then answer the questions.

Exodus 24:3–11—The LORD, through Moses, ratifies His covenant with His people. The Book of the Covenant is read and the people agree to its stipulations. The covenant is sealed with the sprinkling of blood, and God and His people share a covenant meal.

1 Corinthians 10:16–17—St. Paul states that when people share the cup and the bread of the Lord's Supper, they share also the body and blood of Christ and are united to Him.

Mark 14:16–26—During the course of the Passover meal with His disciples, Jesus institutes the Lord's Supper.

1. In the Old Testament lesson, twice the people of God say that they will obey all that the LORD has commanded (verses 3 and 7). Were they able to keep their promise? Why or why not?

2. Why is blood collected from the sacrifices and then sprinkled both upon the altar and upon the people? For help, see Hebrew 9:16–22.

3. What significance can be attached to the fact that after the covenant was ratified with the sprinkling of blood, Moses, Aaron,

45

Nadab, Abihu, and 70 elders ate a meal in the presence of God? For help, remember God's earlier instructions to Moses, recorded in Exodus 19:20–22.

4. In the Epistle lesson, St. Paul emphasizes unity. How is this unity expressed in regard to the Lord's Supper?

5. In the Gospel lesson, Mark tells us that Jesus instituted the Lord's Supper during the Feast of Unleavened Bread. What is the Feast of Unleavened Bread? When was it first celebrated? What significant activities were associated with this ceremony? What is the meaning of this ceremony?

6. What points of comparison are there between the original Passover celebration and the Lord's Supper?

7. What did Jesus mean in calling the cup "the blood of the covenant"? For help, refer to question 2 and Hebrews 9:15–22.

8. What did Jesus mean when He said, "I will not drink again of the fruit of the vine until that day when I drink it anew in the kingdom of God"? For help, see Isaiah 25:6–9 and Luke 14:15–23.

Connect

1. When Adam and Eve sinned against God in Eden, their righteous relationship with God was broken. They hid in shame from His presence and suffered His punishment. Moreover, human relationships also were fractured by evil, a point exemplified in the fact that Cain, the first child born to Adam and Eve, killed his brother Abel. How are the effects of sin apparent today among families and friends? Among congregations? In the way people behave toward God?

2. When you come to the Lord's Supper, what promise does God make to you in Christ? How does He make this promise? How might this promise affect the relationships you have with others who kneel with you at the Table of the Lord? How might it affect the relations between people who have hurt each other or are angry with each other?

3. When God would speak through the prophets about His heavenly kingdom, He would sometimes employ pictures from everyday life. Why would the picture of a great banquet be especially appropriate to describe the blessings of heaven? What hope does such a picture provide for people who have lost loved ones in death, who are separated by distance, or who are forsaken by loved ones entirely?

4. Anna is an elderly lady. Although she is alert, she cannot take adequate care of herself. Her husband died five years ago, and she only had two children, a son and a daughter, who rarely come to see her. For this reason Anna is often depressed and sad, especially when she remembers the days when she and her husband

lived together with their children in a small country home. How might you encourage Anna on the basis of what you have learned in the lessons for today? Write a short note to Anna. Share your note with the group.

Vision

To Do This Week

1. Attend the Lord's Supper. Remember Christ offers Himself in the bread and wine for forgiveness of sins and assures you of your place at the heavenly banquet with all your loved ones in the family of God.
2. Plan to eat together regularly with family and/or friends. Conclude your meals with a devotion. Use a devotion book such as *My Devotions* or *Little Visits with Jesus* or simply read from the Bible, using this format: invocation, Scripture reading, prayer, song.
3. Pray for loved ones who are separated from you by distance or personal differences. Write a letter or make a phone call to share and to receive God's love and forgiveness in Christ with this person.

Closing Worship

Sing stanzas 1 and 4 of "Lord Jesus Christ, We Humbly Pray"
> Lord Jesus Christ, we humbly pray
> That we may feast on You today;
> Beneath these forms of bread and wine
> Enrich us with Your grace divine.
>
> One bread, one cup, one body, we,
> Rejoicing in our unity,
> Proclaim Your love until You come
> To bring Your scattered loved ones home.

Scripture Lessons for Good Friday

In preparation for the next session, read Isaiah 52:13–53:12; Hebrews 4:14–16, 5:7–9; and John 19:17–30.

Session 8

Good Friday

Isaiah 52:13–53:12; Hebrews 4:14–16, 5:7–9; John 19:17–30

Focus

Theme: *A Blessed Death*

Law/Gospel Focus

Death destroys all that people hold dear and is the final end of all people. But Christ gained the victory over sin and death on the cross, making death not the end, but the entrance into lasting life in heaven.

Objectives

By the grace of God in Christ we will
1. explore the manner and meaning of Christ's crucifixion;
2. rejoice that Christ gained the victory over sin and death on the cross;
3. give thanks that Christ altered the meaning of our death.

Opening Worship

Leader: In the name of the Father and of the Son and of the Holy Spirit.
Participants: Amen!
Leader: My God, my God, why have You forsaken me?
Participants: Why are You so far from saving me, so far from the words of my groaning?
Leader: All who see me mock me;
Participants: They hurl insults, shaking their heads:
Leader: "He trusts in the LORD; let the LORD rescue him.
Participants: Let Him deliver him, since He delights in him."
Leader: But You, O LORD, be not far off;
Participants: O my Strength, come quickly to help me.
Leader: I will declare Your name to my brothers;

Introduction

Herodotus tells a story about a wealthy and powerful Lydian king named Croesus, who lived in the sixth century B.C. One day Solon, the famous Athenian statesman and lawgiver, visited Croesus' country, and Croesus could not resist showing off his lands, palaces, and treasuries. He then invited Solon to dinner and asked, "Who is the happiest man that you have ever seen?" Croesus supposed himself to be the happiest man and was chagrined when Solon named an Athenian farmer who died in battle, defending his town. Solon went on to explain, "Never count a man happy until you see the manner of his death?"

1. What do you suppose Solon meant?

2. How can a person prepare for his or her own death?

3. Does the death of a loved one make a person look at life differently? How?

Croesus was angry at Solon for thinking so little of his vast power and wealth. But later he learned the truth of Solon's words. Croesus eventually went to war against Cyrus, king of Persia, and was defeated. Herodotus states that when Croesus was tied to the stake and about to be burned alive, he remembered the words of Solon and realized at that moment how all his former power and wealth came to nothing.

Today is "Good Friday," a day when Christians reflect on the crucifixion of Christ. To some it may seem odd that Christians call the day of the Lord's death "good," but when we see the manner of Jesus' death and what His death means, then we are able to say that this day is good indeed. And we are able to look at the death of loved ones and even our own death in Christ in a different light.

Inform

Look at the brief summaries of the Scripture lessons for Good Friday. Then answer the questions.

Isaiah 52:13–53:12—Here the prophet Isaiah tells of the Servant of the Lord, who will suffer and die so that God's people may have forgiveness and life. The way in which Christ would suffer and the meaning of His passion is foretold as clearly in these verses as anywhere else in the Old Testament.

Hebrews 4:14–16, 5:7–9—The author states that we have a perfect High Priest, whom we can approach with confidence.

John 19:17–30—John gives his account of Christ's crucifixion. Jesus the King lays down His life for His people.

1. Isaiah describes a servant who would suffer greatly. Scan the verses and describe how this person would suffer. Why would this person suffer? What would be the result of His sufferings?

2. Referring to question 1, what similarities are there between the servant and Christ? Between the servant's suffering and Christ's suffering? Between the result of the servant's suffering and the result of Christ's suffering?

3. Can any hope be found in these verses? See especially 53:5, 11–12.

4. The author of Hebrews states that we have a "great High Priest." What does the author mention in these verses that qualify Jesus for this position?

5. The author mentions that because of Christ, we can be confident when we are tempted. What does he mean? How are Christ's temptations and our temptations similar? How are they different? What does it mean that Christ gives us mercy and grace in our time of need?

6. Why did Pilate put the notice, "Jesus of Nazareth, King of the Jews" above Jesus' head as He hung on the cross? Why did the Jews protest? Was this an accurate statement to make of Jesus? Why or why not?

7. Several times in this section John stresses that what happened to Jesus fulfilled Scripture. What things does he mention? What part of the Old Testament is John referring to? What new insights can we glean about the death of Christ in this regard?

8. Jesus finally said, "It is finished." What was He talking about? What do we learn about the death of Christ and its significance for us from these words?

Connect

"Never count a man happy until you see the manner of his death."
Thus spoke Solon. Let's apply these words to our lesson.

1. Imagine that you are Pilate trying to explain why Jesus was crucified. What reasons would you give? Would you say that Jesus'
   death was "good"? Considering how He died, what would you say
   about Jesus?

2. Imagine that you are Isaiah trying to explain why Jesus was crucified. In your own words, what would you say? Would you call
   Jesus' death "good"? Considering how He died, what would you
   say about Jesus?

3. Imagine that you are Mary, standing at the foot of the cross. What
   would you be thinking and feeling? Would you call the day on
   which your son died "good"? Considering how He died, what
   would you say about Jesus?

4. Imagine that you are standing at the grave of a loved one who
   believed in Christ. What would you be thinking and feeling?
   Would you call the day on which your loved one died "good"?
   How does God view the death of His children? For help, look at
   Psalm 116:15 and Revelation 14:13.

To Do This Week

Write your own funeral service. What would you want people to say about you? What hymns would you like to sing? What Scripture lessons would you like to be read?

Closing Worship

Sing stanzas 1 and 3 of "Stricken, Smitten, and Afflicted."

Stricken, smitten, and afflicted,
See Him dying on the tree!
This is Christ, by man rejected;
Here, my soul, your Savior see.
He's the long-expected prophet,
David's son, yet David's Lord.
Proofs I see sufficient of it:
He's the true and faithful Word.

You who think of sin but lightly
Nor suppose the evil great
Here may view its nature rightly,
Here its guilt may estimate.
Mark the sacrifice appointed;
See who bears the awful load;
It's the Word, the Lord's Anointed,
Son of Man and Son of God.

Scripture Lessons for the Resurrection of Our Lord

In preparation for the next session, read Isaiah 25:6–9; 1 Corinthians 15:19–28; and Mark 16:1–8.

Session 9

The Resurrection of Our Lord

Isaiah 25:6–9; 1 Corinthians 15:19–28; Mark 16:1–8

Focus

Theme: *The Great Reversal*

Law/Gospel Focus

Death is the curse of sin and has spread to all people from Adam. Christ suffered the curse of sin in our place. In His resurrection we see the promise of our resurrection.

Objectives

By the grace of God in Christ we will
1. give thanks that Jesus came back to life on the third day;
2. describe what the resurrection of Christ means for God's people;
3. rejoice that we are given a new life in Christ.

Opening Worship

Leader: In the name of the Father and of the Son and of the Holy Spirit.

Participants: Amen!

Leader: Shouts of joy and victory resound in the tents of the righteous:

Participants: "The LORD's right hand has done mighty things!

Leader: The LORD's right hand is lifted high;

Participants: The LORD's right hand has done mighty things!"

Leader: I will not die but live,

Participants: And will proclaim what the LORD has done.

Leader: The LORD has chastened me severely,

Participants: But He has not given me over to death.

Leader: Open for me the gates of righteousness;

Participants: I will enter and give thanks to the LORD.

Introduction

Nine months had gone by, and Bill and Sarah were waiting for the birth of a new child. It would be their first. They had paid careful attention at all the childbirth classes and had always gone to the obstetrician together. They were happy when for the first time they heard the baby's heart beating and excited when they saw the child move in the ultrasound video. But occasionally Sarah would also wonder about the pain of childbirth. Finally, three days after the due date, little Michael was born. Sarah would later say that labor was the most difficult thing she had ever experienced; yet she insisted that the day Michael was born was the happiest day of her life.

1. If you are a parent, think for a moment about the birth of your first child. Share what you experienced?

2. The pain of childbirth also brings great blessings. Are there other times when pain and blessing are so closely united?

Today we celebrate the resurrection of Christ, an event which turned the pain and grief of the disciples into wonder and joy. The lessons for today tell us that in Christ's resurrection a great reversal comes to all creation—from suffering and death to joy and life. Indeed, in Christ's resurrection the pain of death itself is reversed by the promise of eternal life in heaven.

Inform

Look at the brief summaries of the Scripture lessons for the Resurrection of Our Lord. Then answer the questions.

Isaiah 25:6–9—Isaiah portrays life in God's heavenly kingdom as a large and sumptuous banquet where God Himself is the host. While the people of God feast on His goodness, God takes away the sorrow, sin, and death itself.

1 Corinthians 15:19–28—St. Paul assures the believers at Corinth that because Christ is risen from the dead, their bodies too will rise to new life. Paul indicates the sequence of events for this wonderful occurrence.

Mark 16:1–8—On their way to the tomb, Mary Magdalene, Mary the mother of James, and Salome discover that the stone has been rolled away. A "young man" tells them that Jesus has come back to life and will meet the rest of His disciples in Galilee.

1. In the Old Testament lesson, Isaiah talks about a banquet. Where will this banquet take place? For help see Isaiah 2:2–4 and Revelation 19:9. Who will be invited to this banquet? For help, see also Matthew 22:8–10.

2. Isaiah refers to three things in verse 8 that happen to people as a result of sin. What are they? How will God respond to each problem in His heavenly kingdom? Isaiah also presents a contrast between what the people of God eat and what God Himself swallows. What is the contrast?

3. Remember that Isaiah addressed these words to people who would eventually be taken into exile. They would lose their homes, many of their loved ones, their homeland, and be taken forcibly to a foreign land. Why would God do this to the Israelites? Yet God in this image provides words of comfort. Why would an image of a heavenly banquet be so appropriate for the Israelites? What else does Isaiah say that would bring them comfort?

4. In the Epistle lesson, St. Paul presents a contrast between Adam and Christ. What came through Adam? How did this happen? What comes through Christ? When will this happen? For help, see Genesis 1:15–17 and Romans 5:12. See also 1 Thessalonians 4:13–17.

5. Paul states that if Christ has not risen from the dead, then believers in Christ are "to be pitied more than all men." Why do you suppose he would say this? For help, see 1 Corinthians 15:14–15.

6. In the Gospel lesson, who was the "young man" who appeared to the women? How did he try to convince them that Jesus had come back to life?

7. What other details are recorded about the resurrection of Christ? For help, see Matthew 28:1–4, 8–15 and John 20:1–18.

═══ Connect ═══

1. Paul stated that without belief in the resurrection of Christ, Christianity makes no sense and Christians are "miserable" people. Yet this event has often been questioned or denied by opponents of Christianity. How would you answer these common statements directed against the resurrection?

a. Christ never rose. The grave was never empty. Instead, the disciples fabricated the whole story.

b. The grave was empty, but the disciples stole the body of Christ and then invented the story.

c. Jesus didn't really die on the cross. He "swooned" and later, after reviving, came out of the tomb and appeared to people.

d. The Pharisees removed the body and the disciples, seeing the grave was empty, mistakenly thought Jesus had come back to life.

2. Because of Christ's resurrection, the effects of sin have been reversed. Christ has gained the victory over suffering and death. Death is no longer the end. How does God now view the death of His people? For help look at Psalm 116:15 and Revelation 14:13. Is their any similarity between how God views the death of His children with how people view the birth of a child?

3. But also look at John 11:33–35. Jesus knew He was going to raise Lazarus from death. Why did He weep? How does this passage together with the passages in question 2 alter how we view the death of a loved one? For help, see Romans 8:22–25.

4. Remember that Isaiah wrote to people whose families would suffer and be fragmented by an invading enemy. What enemies exist today that fragment families? What promises does God bring in Isaiah to fragmented families?

5. George's wife was recently diagnosed with terminal cancer. The doctors say she may live for four more weeks, but not much beyond that. George and his wife were both baptized and remain lifelong Christians. Take a few moments to write a short note to George. Then consider reading your note to the group.

Vision

To Do This Week

1. Take time this week to think of loved ones who have died in Christ. Read again the passage in Isaiah and how it applies to your reunion with this loved one in heaven. In your prayers, thank God for this hope.
2. If you know someone who grieves the loss of a loved one, consider how you might share with them the hope that comes in Christ's resurrection.

Closing Worship

Sing stanzas 1 and 7 of "I Know that My Redeemer Lives."
>I know that my Redeemer lives!
>What comfort this sweet sentence gives!
>He lives, He lives, who once was dead;
>He lives, my ever-living head!
>
>He lives and grants me daily breath;
>He lives, and I shall conquer death;
>He lives my mansion to prepare;
>He lives to bring me safely there.

Scripture Lessons for the Second Sunday of Easter

In preparation for the next session, read Acts 3:13–26, 1 John 5:1–6, and John 20:19–31.

Session 10

Second Sunday of Easter

Acts 3:13–26; 1 John 5:1–6; John 20:19–31

Focus

Theme: *The Name of Jesus*

Law/Gospel Focus

In the Second Commandment God requires that people not misuse His name. Yet the name of God is often misunderstood, neglected, or invoked for sinful reasons. But at the name of Jesus God grants forgiveness, healing, and life.

Objectives

By the grace of God in Christ we will
1. describe the meaning of the name *Jesus;*
2. recognize the blessings that come from God to us in Jesus' name;
3. explain how the people of God rightly call upon the name of Christ.

Opening Worship

Leader: In the name of the Father and of the Son and of the Holy Spirit.

Participants: Amen!

Leader: Give thanks to the LORD, call on His name;

Participants: Make known among the nations what He has done.

Leader: Sing to Him, sing praise to Him;

Participants: Tell of all His wonderful acts.

Leader: Glory in His holy name;

Participants: Let the hearts of those who seek the LORD rejoice.

Leader: Look to the LORD and His strength;

Participants: Seek His face always.

> Leader: Remember the wonders He had done,
> Participants: The miracles, and the judgments He
>   pronounced.
> Leader: He is the LORD our God;
> Participants: His judgments are in all the earth.
> Leader: He remembers His covenant forever,
> Participants: The word He commanded, for a thousand gener-
>   ations.
>   (Psalm 105:1–5, 7–8)

Introduction

One often finds in the Bible that a person's name indicates something about his character. Jacob's name, for example, meant "Grabber," a name given at birth which also became an apt description of how he dealt with his immediate family, Laban, and even with God. His name was later changed to "Israel," which means "he contends with God," when Jacob learned the importance of going to God in prayer and holding Him to His gracious promises. Abram's name, "exalted father," was changed by God to Abraham, "father of many," to indicate how God would multiply his descendants into a great nation. But by far the most important name in the Bible is "Jesus."

1. What do you suppose people, believers and unbelievers alike, think when they hear the name *Jesus?*

2. How do people use the name *Jesus?*

3. Judging by how Jesus' name is used, what might a person think the name means? What conclusions might one make about Jesus as a person?

When the angel Gabriel visited Joseph, the angel stated Joseph was to name Mary's child Jesus because "He will save His people from their sins" (Matthew 1:21). Jesus means "Savior," a name which certainly describes His character. In this session we will learn more about this wonderful name and how God grants blessings to those who call upon it.

Inform

Look at the brief summaries of the Scripture lessons for the Second Sunday of Easter. Then answer the questions.

Acts 3:13–26—For the entire Easter season, readings from the book of Acts take the place of the Old Testament reading. This should not imply that the Old Testament is any less important than the New Testament. Rather, the intent is to trace how God in Christ continued to establish a community of believers after Christ ascended into heaven. It is important to remember that the promise of a Savior is repeated throughout Scripture, beginning in Genesis 3. First, the promise was given to Adam, later to the patriarchs, then illumined by the prophets and finally proclaimed and revealed by Christ among the Jews, and spread by the apostles throughout the world. All the saints were justified by faith in this promise, not by their our attrition or contrition. Here Luke recounts a speech made by Peter immediately after he healed a crippled man. Peter states that not only this miracle, but salvation for all people comes through the name of Jesus.

1 John 5:1–6—John writes on the themes of faith, rebirth, love, obedience, and victory. By faith in Jesus a person becomes a child of God and overcomes the world.

John 20:19–31—Jesus appears to His disciples after the resurrection and again grants them the authority to pronounce forgiveness of sins. Thomas, who was not present, doubts the resurrection but later worships Jesus as his "God" after touching the living Christ's hands and side.

1. The brief sermon by Peter was prompted by an incident. What was it? See verses 1–11. How was it possible that this could happen? See especially verses 12 and 16.

2. What does Peter say about Jesus in his address?

3. In the second lesson John mentions two things that happen for people who have faith in Jesus' name. What are they?

   a. When and how does the first thing happen? For help, see also John 3:3–5, Titus 3:5, and Romans 8:15–16.

   b. How and when does the second thing happen? For help, look at the following verses:
   1 Corinthians 15:56–57

   Romans 8:1

   Romans 5:1–5

4. In the Gospel lesson Jesus gave the disciples authority to forgive and retain sin. When else had He done this? See Matthew 16:13–19. How do the people of God exercise this authority?

5. Why do you suppose Thomas refused to believe the other disciples? What did Thomas say about Jesus after he touched His hands and side? What did Jesus then say to Thomas?

Connect

1. The name *Jesus* means Savior. Look through the lessons again and make a list of how salvation comes to those who have faith in Christ's name.

2. How is the name of Jesus employed in Christian worship? How might you uphold the name of Jesus at home? At school? At work?

3. Mary and John had been married for a number of years and wanted to have children. The pastor of their nondenominational church told them to pray to God. The pastor had said that Jesus once told His disciples, "You may ask Me for anything in My name, and I will do it" (John 14:14). So Mary and John prayed, but she never became pregnant. When they spoke again to their pastor, he indicated that they needed to "believe and not doubt" (James 1:6) because a person who doubted God would not receive anything. Mary and John tried to exercise their faith. They made a nursery and she even "in faith" began to wear maternity clothes. Still she did not become pregnant. Eventually Mary and John became disillusioned and left their church.

   a. Did this pastor given John and Mary good advice? What might he have said differently?

   b. How should Christians understand Jesus' words in John 14:14? Are their any limits to what they can and should request? How does what you have learned about the name of Jesus help you to understand this verse?

c. Had the pastor quoted James 1:6 correctly? Why or why not?

d. What might you now say to Mary and John?

Vision

To Do This Week

1. During your meditation this week, think of what impression you give to people about Jesus by the things you say and do. Write on a piece of paper the times you failed to give a Christian witness. Confess these to the heavenly Father and then at the bottom of the page write, "In the name of Jesus Christ, I am forgiven."
2. Make another list of how you might call upon the name of Jesus and also teach others to do so. Pray that God would enable you to do these things.

Closing Worship

Sing stanzas 1 and 2 of "How Sweet the Name of Jesus Sounds."
How sweet the name of Jesus sounds
In a believer's ear!
It soothes our sorrows, heals our wounds,
And drives away all fear.

It makes the wounded spirit whole
And calms the heart's unrest;
It's manna to the hungry soul
And to the weary, rest.

Scripture Lessons for the Third Sunday of Easter

In preparation for the next session, read Acts 4:8–12, 1 John 1:1–2:2, and Luke 24:36–49.

Session 11

Third Sunday of Easter

Acts 4:8–12; 1 John 1:1–2:2; Luke 24:36–49

Focus

Theme: *Walking in the Light*

Law/Gospel Focus

Those who desire life with God must live in the truth, confessing their own true nature and boldly proclaiming God's word to others. Yet because of sin, we are afraid and ashamed of the truth. God in Christ takes away our shame and grants us boldness to be Christ's witnesses.

Objectives

By the grace of God in Christ we will
1. explore what it to means to have lives filled with integrity and truth before God;
2. discover where the people of God find boldness to proclaim the truth;
3. give thanks that when we confess sins, God forgives us in Christ;
4. thank God for empowering His Gospel to bring life to us and those around us.

Opening Worship

Leader: In the name of the Father and of the Son and of the Holy Spirit.

Participants: Amen!

Leader: I will sing of the LORD's great love forever;

Participants: With my mouth I will make Your faithfulness known through all generations.

Leader: Righteousness and justice are the foundation of Your throne;

Introduction

Light can hurt. One day while camping with the family, my son and I decided to try out our new flashlight. The package stated that the beam would shine out to one quarter of a mile, and we wanted to know if this was true. So we ventured into the woods on a black, moonless night. Neither one of us could see the other, and my son was fumbling around trying to find the switch for the high powered beam. I was just bending over to help him when that one-quarter-mile beam suddenly flared to life, blazing right into my eyes, two feet away. Light can hurt! More often, however, light hurts because it exposes defects. Before his televised presidential campaign debate with John Kennedy, Richard Nixon refused to have makeup applied to his face. As a result he looked nervous and less "presidential" on camera, and many thought this contributed not only to the loss of the debate but also to his loss of the presidential election in 1960. On the other hand, light can be a blessing. It guides people through dark places, provides knowledge of one's surroundings, and leads to the discovery of new ideas.

1. When did you find light to be extraordinarily helpful? Was there ever a time when light was painful?

2. In the Bible, light is a metaphor for truth as well as righteousness and life. On what occasions is the truth extraordinarily helpful? When do people find the truth painful?

John states, "God is light; in Him there is no darkness at all" (1 John 1:5). During the course of this lesson we will consider what this means, how people react to God's light, and how in Christ this light becomes a wonderful, life-giving blessing.

Inform

Look at the brief summaries of the Scripture lessons for the Third Sunday of Easter. Then answer the questions.

Acts 4:8–12—Luke continues telling what happened after Peter healed the crippled man. Peter and John were taken before the Sanhedrin, where Peter testified about Jesus Christ.

1 John 1:1–2:2—John states that fellowship with God means living in the "light." The people of God thus receive forgiveness and life.

Luke 24:36–49—Jesus appears to the disciples and convinces them that He has indeed risen from the dead. He gives them power to understand the Scriptures and tells them to wait for the promised Holy Spirit.

1. In Acts, Luke tells us that after Peter healed the crippled man, he and John were taken before the Sanhedrin. This was the same ruling council in Jerusalem that only a little while ago had put Jesus on trial and sent Him on to Pilate. Caiaphas, who had previously charged Jesus with "blasphemy" before the council, was again present. If you were Peter, how would you feel about being questioned by the Sanhedrin? Why would you feel this way? What did Peter say on such an occasion? Do his words tell us anything about the way he might have felt?

2. Remember also that this was not the first time Peter had stood in the presence of the Sanhedrin. Read about the other time in Mark 14:66–72. What did Peter do the first time? What has happened to Peter to make such a great change? For help, look at verse 8. See also Acts 1:8 and Matthew 10:19–20.

3. In the second lesson, John begins his letter by referring to his qualifications as a witness for the "Word of life." Who is the Word of life? For help, see John 1:1 and 1:14. Looking at these verses, what makes John such a good witness for this person?

4. John then describes God by way of a metaphor—light. What do you suppose John intends to convey by this metaphor. What is stated in verse 7? What is implied in verses 8–10? See also Ephesians 5:8–14 and 2 Corinthians 4:6.

5. In verses 8–10 John characterizes the behavior of those who dwell in the light and those who dwell in the darkness. What does he say? For help, see also John 3:19–21. How does God treat those who in this manner come into the light? See verse 7 and verse 9. How does Jesus react to those who come into the light? Look at 2:1–2. What happens to those who refuse to come into the light?

6. In the Gospel the disciples apparently had a hard time believing that Jesus Christ had actually come back to life. At first Jesus tried to convince them by having them touch His body and by eating food in their presence, something which a "ghost" would not do. But then He also convinced them in another way. How?

7. Jesus then told the disciples to stay in the city until they had been "clothed with power from on high"? To what event is Jesus refer-

ring? Why was it so important for the disciples to wait for what the "Father has promised"?

Connect

1. Just as actual light can be painful, so too can God's light be painful. How is this so? For help, look again at John 3:19–21. Can you think of an example in the Bible where people hid from the light of God's presence? Why did they do this? How do people today avoid God's "light"? How will evil people react when Christ comes again in glory? For help, see Revelation 6:15–17.

2. When God's light shines into the human heart, what is exposed? For help, see Mark 7:21–23. What did Christ do to make God's holy light a healing light? How do we come into this healing light? Refer to 1 John 1:9–10. See also 1 Corinthians 2:14 and 12:3. How can we bring this healing light to others?

3. When Jesus showed Himself to the disciples, He presented physical evidence and scriptural evidence that He had risen from the dead. What kind of evidence do believers in Christ now have to show that Jesus has risen from the dead and is the Savior?

   a. Obviously we cannot point to the resurrected body of Christ, but is there any other physical or tangible evidence that points to the resurrection of Christ so that people will come into the light of God's grace? For help, look at Matthew 5:14–16. What evidence

71

did Peter have at his disposal before the Sanhedrin? What evidence is at your congregation's disposal? What evidence might you provide at work, school, or home?

b. We also have another means at our disposal to convince people that Jesus is the Savior of all so that they will come into the light of salvation. What is it? For help, see Psalm 119:105 and 2 Peter 1:19.

4. What can believers in Christ do to become more effective "light-bearers"? In your answer refer to question 3 above. But also think of how Peter became a more effective "light-bearer" before the Sanhedrin? For help, see Matthew 10:19–20, John 16:12–15, and Acts 1:8.

Vision

To Do This Week

1. Write the words of 1 John 1:8–9 on the back of a 3 × 5 card. During your devotions this week, ask God to shine His light from His Word into your heart. When you become aware of sins, confess them before God and read the words of 1 John 1:8–9.
2. Dwelling in God's light means that we are also truthful with others in the way in which we confess sin and receive each others' forgiveness. In your devotions this week, consider your relationships with loved ones. Where necessary, confess sin and ask for forgiveness.
3. On another three by five card, write three things you might do or say this week to become a more effective light-bearer in the world. Ask that the Holy Spirit would accomplish through these three items what you are unable to do by yourself.

Closing Worship

Sing stanzas 1 and 3 of "O Word of God Incarnate."

O Word of God incarnate, O Wisdom from on high,
O Truth unchanged, unchanging, O Light of our dark sky:
We praise You for the radiance That from the hallowed
    page,
A lantern to our footsteps, Shines on from age to age.

Oh, make Your Church, dear Savior, A lamp of burnished
    gold
To bear before the nations Your true light as of old!
Oh, teach Your wand'ring pilgrims By this their path to trace
Till, clouds and darkness ended, They see You face to face!

Scripture Lessons for the Fourth Sunday of Easter

In preparation for the next session, read Acts 4:23–33, 1 John
3:1–2, and John 10:11–18.

Session 12

Fourth Sunday of Easter

Acts 4:23–33; 1 John 3:1–2; John 10:11–18

Focus

Theme: *The Shepherd King*

Law/Gospel Focus

God has made Christ the king over all peoples, yet we often rebel from His authority because of our own sin and the sin of others. Yet Christ is a "Shepherd King" who graciously seeks those who are lost and protects them from danger.

Objectives

By the power of the Holy Spirit working through God's Word we will
1. understand more clearly what Jesus meant when He claimed to be the "Good Shepherd";
2. affirm that Christ is a powerful king over all people;
3. confess that Christ is a gracious king for believers.

Opening Worship

Leader: In the name of the Father and of the Son and of the Holy Spirit.
Participants: Amen!
Leader: This is what the Sovereign LORD says:
Participants: I myself will search for My sheep and look after them.
Leader: As a shepherd looks after his scattered flock when he is with them,
Participants: So will I look after My sheep.
Leader: I will rescue them from all the places where they were scattered,
Participants: [Where they were scattered] on a day of clouds and darkness.

Leader:	I will bring them out from the nations and gather them from the countries,
Participants:	And I will bring them into their own land.
Leader:	I will search for the lost and bring back the strays.
Participants:	I will bind up the injured and strengthen the weak.
Leader:	I will make a covenant of peace with them and rid the land of wild beasts
Participants:	So that they may live in the desert and sleep in the forests in safety.
Leader:	They will know that I am the LORD, when I break the bars of their yoke
Participants:	And rescue them from the hands of those who enslaved them.

(Adapted from Ezekiel 34:11–13, 16, 25, 27)

Introduction

In the Gospel lesson for today, Jesus calls Himself the "Good Shepherd." Among a shepherd's duties in the ancient Near East were finding grass and water for the sheep. During times of drought this was often difficult. The shepherd was also charged with protecting the flock from harsh weather and predators. These duties often kept shepherds away from their own dwellings for extended periods. The shepherd's task was often complicated by the sheep, which are generally defenseless before predators and lack self-preservation abilities to the point where they easily become lost.

Both "shepherd" and "sheep" are also metaphors in the ancient world for the relationship between a ruler and his people. An ancient king's duties included providing for his people and protecting them from danger.

1. Where do people seek protection?

2. Upon whom do people generally rely to meet their needs?

In the modern world, government agencies are given duties to protect and provide for the needs of the citizens. The lessons for this week, however, direct our attention to our needs before God and the enemies of our faith and salvation. They direct us to trust in Jesus, the Good Shepherd.

Inform

Look at the brief summaries of the Scripture lessons for the Fourth Sunday of Easter. Then answer the questions.

Acts 4:23–33— Luke concludes his narrative about the healing of the crippled man and the witness given by the Peter and John. Upon their release by the Sanhedrin, they return to the group of believers and pray for boldness and power, so that Christ's name may be upheld.

1 John 3:1–2—John affirms that because of God's great love in Christ, we have become children of God and will share in the glory of His Son.

John 10:11–18—Jesus describes Himself as the Good Shepherd of God's people. He thus describes what kind of king He is for the people of God.

1. The Sanhedrin had threatened Peter and John and commanded them never to speak to anyone in the name of Jesus again. Then the Sanhedrin let them go (Acts 4:17–22). Peter and John returned to their own people, with whom they prayed. What did they ask for in prayer? What happened after they prayed?

2. In prayer the believers quoted Psalm 2.
   a. Find this psalm in your Bible and read it. What is this psalm about? Who is the Lord's anointed? See especially verse 7. Where else in the Bible were these words spoken? What does God think of those who conspire against His Anointed One? How is the authority of the Anointed One described? Are there any limits to His kingdom? For help see also Matthew 28:18 and Philippians 2:9–11.

76

b. What similarities are there between this psalm and what had happened to Peter and John? How might Peter, John, and the rest of the believers have been comforted by the words of this psalm?

3. In the second lesson John states that believers are children of God, yet the world does not recognize them as such. He gives two reasons for this. What are they? For help, see also John 8:15–21 and Colossians 3:3–4. When will it become evident to all that believers are children of God?

4. In the Gospel lesson Jesus stated that He is the Good Shepherd. a. The sheep are the people of God. What needs do they have before God? Are they, like sheep, prone to become lost and go astray if left to themselves? How does God provide for these needs? For help see John 10:28 and Isaiah 53:5–6.

b. Continuing the metaphor, who is the wolf? For help, see Ephesians 6:10–12, 1 Peter 5:8–9, Acts 20:29–30, and Matthew 7:17. How does Jesus, our Shepherd, protect us against these enemies? For help, look at verse 7 of the text and also 1 John 5:4–5 and John 14:26.

5. What else does Jesus say about Himself by claiming to be the Good Shepherd? For help, look at Psalm 23 and also Ezekiel 34. Make a list of characteristics.

Connect

1. From the first lesson we learn that Jesus is the King over all creation. His enemies cannot oppose Him. How are the church and the people of God attacked by enemies in society? By enemies within civil government? By enemies even within the visible church and the local congregation? How can the people of God fight against these enemies? Where will they find the victory over these enemies?

2. From the Gospel lesson we learn that Jesus the King wants to be a Shepherd King. Jesus said, "My sheep know Me." What does it mean to "know" Christ? For help, consider what the Sanhedrin knew about Christ. Yet did they know Christ in the same way His sheep know Him? What is the difference between the two? For help, see also Philippians 3:10. How can believers bring others to "know" the Shepherd at work or school? At a congregation?

3. Jesus also said, "My sheep listen to My voice; … and they follow Me" (John 10:27). How do believers hear the voice of Jesus? How do they follow their Shepherd?

Vision

To Do This Week

Remembering that Jesus is your Shepherd, make a list of all the ways that Jesus cares for you, His lamb.

Closing Worship

Sing stanzas 1 and 6 of "The King of Love My Shepherd Is."

> The King of love my Shepherd is,
> Whose goodness faileth never;
> I nothing lack if I am His
> And He is mine forever.

> And so through all the length of days
> Thy goodness faileth never.
> Good Shepherd, may I sing Thy praise
> Within Thy house forever.

Scripture Lessons for the Fifth Sunday of Easter

In preparation for the next session, read Acts 8:26–40, 1 John 3:18–24, and John 15:1–8.

Session 13

Fifth Sunday of Easter

Acts 8:26–40; 1 John 3:18–24; John 15:1–8

Focus

Theme: *Life on the Vine*

Law/Gospel Focus

Believers are called to love God and one another not only in word but also in deed. Apart from Christ they are dead in sin and can accomplish nothing good. But God unites believers to Christ through faith and then makes their lives outwardly and inwardly fruitful.

Objectives

By the grace of God in Christ we will

1. describe what it means to be attached to Christ and bear fruit;
2. affirm how God through the Holy Spirit graciously empowers our words and deeds, which are done in faith, for His gracious purposes.

Opening Worship

Leader: In the name of the Father and of the Son and of the Holy Spirit.
Participants: Amen!
Leader: The Lord is faithful to all His promises
Participants: And loving toward all He has made.
Leader: The Lord upholds all those who fall
Participants: And lifts up all who are bowed down.
Leader: The Lord is righteous in all His ways
Participants: And loving toward all He has made.
Leader: The Lord is near to all who call on Him,
Participants: To all who call on Him in truth.

Introduction

A friend of mine, Sharon, once told me about a time when she was ill at the age of five. She had just had an operation and would have to remain in the hospital for a few days. During that time she remembers how a Catholic nun, Sister Matilda, came several times to cheer her up. Matilda would smile and chat and pray and then leave a small toy. She visited Sharon twice before Sharon went home. That all happened 32 years ago, yet Sister Matilda's words and smile left such a large impact upon Sharon that she remembers it as if it were only yesterday.

1. Describe a time when someone's simple activity, or words, had a powerful and positive influence upon you.

2. Why did this person have such an impact on you?

3. What makes a person's words or activity affect another's life?

The lessons for today show how God makes our lives fruitful in Christ. By God's grace through faith believers are united to Christ, and their lives begin to reflect His blessings. The Holy Spirit also uses them to bless the lives of others.

Inform

Look at the brief summaries of the Scripture lessons for the Fifth Sunday of Easter. Then answer the questions.

Acts 8:26–40—The Holy Spirit leads Philip to an Ethiopian eunuch, who asks about a passage found in Isaiah. After telling him about Jesus Christ, Philip baptized the eunuch and then was led away by the Holy Spirit to evangelize elsewhere.

1 John 3:18–24—St. John connects love for Christ and others with obedience to His commands.

John 15:1–8—Jesus describes the disciples' lives as branches that have been attached to a vine and bear much fruit.

1. Acts 8 marks a transition in the growth of the New Testament church. Up to this point the believers had largely evangelized only fellow Jews. But then something happened to bring the Gospel to those who were generally avoided or disdained by Jews. What was this event? For help read 8:1–8. Who were the "despised" people who heard the Gospel?

2. Was the Ethiopian eunuch also disdained by the Jewish religious leaders? For help see Deuteronomy 23:1. Yet what had God through Isaiah said about Eunuchs in Isaiah 56:3–7? What does this tell you about the grace and love of God in Christ?

3. The Acts of the Apostles is sometimes referred to as "The Acts of the Holy Spirit." How was the Holy Spirit instrumental in this entire episode? Would you say the Holy Spirit similarly empowers the witness of all His people, or is Philip unique?

4. In the second lesson, how does St. John connect love and obedience? Obedience and a good conscience? Obedience and unity with Christ? For help, see also Ephesians 2:10 and John 15:10–11.

5. In the Gospel lesson, John talks about bearing fruit. What are the characteristics of a "fruitful" life? For help, see Colossians 1:10 and Galatians 5:22.

6. John states that a person must "remain" in Christ in order to be fruitful. What does he mean? For help, see John 15:3 and also 1 John 4:13–16.

Connect

1. In a prayer St. Augustine wrote, "Our hearts are restless until they rest in Thee." By that he meant the human heart will not find peace until it comes to know and worship God through Jesus Christ. Do you agree or disagree with St. Augustine?

2. What are some commonly held characteristics of a fruitful life in your community? How do these characteristics compare with those found in Scripture?

3. Believers, who are part of the vine, bear fruit even through suffering. St. Paul wrote that "in all things God works for the good of those who love Him, who have been called according to His purpose" (Romans 8:28). How is this truth illustrated in the lesson

recorded in Acts? What event can you recall, which at the time was filled with suffering or hardship, but which God used to strengthen your faith or to bring others to faith?

4. Believers and congregations, which are part of the vine, also have fruitful ministry. Considering how Jesus said, "Neither can you bear fruit unless you remain in Me," what ought to be the priorities of congregations that desire to have fruitful ministries? Make a list of items that focus on "remaining" in Christ. How can an individual "remain" in Christ? A family?

5. Congregations and individuals may sometimes wonder whether their witness in word and deed is having any impact on a community, associates, friends, or loved ones. If they see little change, they may be tempted to despair. What comfort can be found from the role that the Holy Spirit plays in Acts?

6. Sister Matilda also may have wondered from time to time whether she was having any impact on the people she visited. If you were Sharon, how would you encourage her never to give up but to always trust that God was graciously using her words and deeds? What encouraging thing might she say from Scripture? What might she say about her own experience? Write a note to Sister Matilda and then consider reading your note to the group.

Vision

To Do This Week

1. Think of someone in your congregation who has been influential in helping you grow in the faith. What have they done? How have they helped you? Write a note of thanks and encouragement to this person.

2. Consider how you might tell others about the love and forgiveness of Christ by what you do and say. Make a list on a 3 × 5 card. On the reverse side of the card write the words of Acts 1:8. Place this card in a prominent place so that each day you may be reminded of how the Holy Spirit will empower your words and deeds even in ways of which you are not aware.

Closing Worship

Sing stanzas 1, 2 and 4 of "Christ Is Our Cornerstone"

Christ is our cornerstone,
On Him alone we build;
With His true saints alone
The courts of heav'n are filled.
On His great love Our hopes we place
Of present grace And joys above.

Oh, then, with hymns of praise
These hallowed courts shall ring;
Our voices we will raise
The Three in One to sing
And thus proclaim In joyful song,
Both loud and long, That glorious name.

Here may we gain from heav'n
The grace which we implore,
And may that grace, once giv'n,
Be with us evermore
Until that day When all the blest
To endless rest Are called away.

Scripture Lessons for the Sixth Sunday of Easter

In preparation for the next session, read Acts 11:19–30, 1 John 4:1–11, and John 15:9–17.

Session 14

Sixth Sunday of Easter

Acts 11:19–30; 1 John 4:1–11; John 15:9–17

Focus

Theme: *The Language of Love*

Law/Gospel Focus

Jesus commands us to love each other as He has loved us. Jesus not only demonstrates how we ought to love each other, but also in love forgives our sin and creates His love in our hearts through the Holy Spirit.

Objectives

By the grace of God in Christ we will

1. understand more clearly what Christ meant when He commanded His followers to "love" each other;
2. affirm our inability to love as God commands;
3. give thanks that Christ demonstrates God's love for us;
4. trust in God to create Christ's love in our hearts so that we love others.

Opening Worship

Leader: In the name of the Father and of the Son and of the Holy Spirit.

Participants: Amen!

Leader: The LORD is compassionate and gracious,

Participants: Slow to anger, abounding in love.

Leader: He will not always accuse,

Participants: Nor will He harbor His anger forever;

Leader: He does not treat us as our sins deserve

Participants: Or repay us according to our iniquities.

Leader: For as high as the heavens are above the earth,

Participants: So great is His love for those who fear Him;

Introduction

In today's Gospel lesson Jesus commands His followers to love each other. Love is such an integral part of a believer's life that Jesus made it a distinguishing characteristic. "By this all men will know that you are My disciples, if you love one another" (John 13:35). Yet while even many unbelievers understand that Christians are to love others, what Jesus meant by this command is often misunderstood. Part of the problem is that "love" is an English word which describes many things.

1. What do people commonly mean by the following statements?
    a. "I love football."

    b. "I love my spouse."

    c. "I fell in love."

2. How do believers in a congregation show their "love" for each other? For others in the community? At school or at work?

Jesus did not merely command His followers to love each other, He modeled that love Himself. More important, He demonstrated that love for us.

Inform

Look at the summaries of the Scripture lessons for the Sixth Sunday of Easter. Then answer the questions.

Acts 11:19–30—Believers spread the Gospel among the Greek people at Antioch. When the church leaders in Jerusalem heard of this, they sent Barnabas to encourage the new converts. The latter respond in kind by helping the saints in Jerusalem during a famine.

1 John 4:1–11—John sets forth the distinguishing characteristics of those who are from God.

John 15:9–17—During the course of the Last Supper, Jesus exhorts His disciples to love each other as He has loved them.

1. In Acts, Luke identifies three notable developments in the spread of Christianity. The Gospel is preached to Greek people (verse 20); Saul becomes involved in evangelizing Greek people (verse 25ff.); and Antioch becomes an early center of Gentile Christianity (verse 26). Why are these events so significant?

2. Jewish and Gentile people at this time would usually not associate with each other. They had different philosophies, customs, and beliefs. How did the Jewish and Gentile Christians show their love and support for each other? What made the difference for the Jewish and Gentile people in this part of Acts? For help, see Galatians 3:28 and Ephesians 2:14–16.

3. In the second lesson, John identifies four characteristics of those who are "from God." What are they? Look at verses 2–3, verse 4, verse 6, and verse 7.

4. How does John define love? See especially verse 10.

5. In the Gospel lesson, John identifies two other distinguishing characteristics of divine love. What are they? See especially verse 10 and verse 13.

Connect

1. The distinguishing characteristics of agape love are self-sacrifice, forgiveness, and faithfulness. How can the people of God show agape love? For help, look at the following passages.
Matthew 18:21–22

   Matthew 5:38–42

   John 14:15

   Matthew 5:43–48

2. Look again at the list above. How does God's standard of love compare with what we see and learn of love from the media? From society? How does it compare with what we see happening in homes? How does it compare with what we see in our own hearts?

3. Love is expressed in visible and tangible ways. In what visible and tangible manner did God show His love for people? For help, see Romans 5:8. How did the believers at Antioch respond to God's

love in Christ and to their fellow Christians in Judea? What are some visible and tangible ways in which your congregation can respond to God's love in Christ and demonstrate love to people in your community?

4. Do people who love each other ever get angry at each other? Can love and anger coexist? When believers become angry at each other, what should they do? For help, see Ephesians 4:26, James 5:16, and Matthew 18:15.

Vision

To Do This Week

1. For devotions, read 1 Corinthians 13. Reread verses 4–7, substituting the word *Jesus* wherever you read the word *love*. Remember that Jesus came to demonstrate this love for you!
2. Also read the parable of the lost son (Luke 15:11–32). How does the father show agape love to both sons? What is the application of this parable?

Closing Worship

Sing stanzas 1, 3, and 5 of "O God of Mercy, God of Light"
O God of mercy, God of light,
In love and mercy infinite,
Teach us, as ever in Your sight,
To live our lives in You.

Teach us the lesson Jesus taught:
To feel for those His blood has bought,
That ev'ry deed and word and thought
May work a work for You.

And may Your Holy Spirit move
All those who live to live in love
Till You receive in heav'n above
Those who have lived to You.

Scripture Lessons for the Ascension of Our Lord

In preparation for the next session, read Acts 1:1–11, Ephesians 1:16–23, and Luke 24:44–53.

Session 15

The Ascension of Our Lord

Acts 1:1–11; Ephesians 1:16–23; Luke 24:44–53

Focus

Theme: *The Second Half*

Law/Gospel Focus

Christ commanded His people to be His witnesses through-out the world. Yet without Christ's anointing we are lost and confused, easily discouraged, and weak and ineffectual. We therefore have no hope of carrying out Christ's last instructions. But Christ Jesus has been glorified and through the Holy Spirit gives believers knowledge, hope, and power.

Objectives

By the grace of God in Christ we will
1. connect the ascension of Christ with His glorification and the sending of the Holy Spirit;
2. affirm how we, who are unable to carry out Christ's last instructions, receive from Christ knowledge, hope, and power;
3. rejoice that Christ will come again to receive His people into a glorious everlasting home.

Opening Worship

Leader: In the name of the Father and of the Son and of the Holy Spirit!
Participants: Amen!
Leader: Then I saw a Lamb, looking as if it had been slain,
Participants: Standing in the center of the throne.
Leader: [And all creation worshiped] the Lamb ...
Participants: And they sang a new song:
Leader: "You are worthy to take the scroll and to open its seals,

Participants: Because You were slain,
Leader: And with Your blood You purchased men for God
Participants: From every tribe and language and people and nation.
Leader: You have made them to be a kingdom and priests to serve our God,
Participants: And they will reign on the earth.
Leader: Worthy is the Lamb, who was slain, to receive power and wealth
Participants: And wisdom and strength and honor and glory and praise!
Leader: To Him who sits on the throne and to the Lamb
Participants: Be praise and honor and glory and power for ever and ever!
Leader: Amen!
Participants: Amen!
            (Adapted from Revelation 5:6–10, 12, 13)

Introduction

During halftime at a basketball or football game, the players and coach will retire to the locker room. There the players will have a brief rest, but more important, the coach will try to prepare his or her players for the second half. The coach will talk about the game plan, perhaps pointing out mistakes that have been made and making adjustments to the offense or defense. The coach will try to rally the players, building up their self-confidence.

1. What is more important for players to hear—a game plan for the second half or a confidence-boosting pep talk? Why?

2. Are there any limits on what a coach can do for the team? If so, what are they?

When Christ entered heaven, the people of God stood on the threshold of a new age. They were entering a time when the Gospel of forgiveness would begin to spread to all corners of the earth, a time marked by Christ's exaltation in glory and the sending of the Holy Spirit, a time which would continue until Judgment Day. Before Christ ascended, He gave the disciples crucial instructions, because they would need knowledge, hope, and power if they were to be His witnesses to all peoples.

Inform

Look at the summaries of the Scripture lessons for the Ascension of Our Lord. Then answer the questions.

Acts 1:1–11—Luke begins the second of his two-part work where he ended the first. Jesus tells the disciples to await the "gift" promised by the Father—the Holy Spirit. They will then receive power and will be Christ's witnesses throughout the world. Having said this, Jesus ascended into heaven.

Ephesians 1:16–23—Paul indicates how he prays for the Ephesians. He asks that God would fill them with wisdom and revelation, with hope, and with power. Christ has been exalted and rules over all things for the sake of the church.

Luke 24:44–53—Luke ends his Gospel with the last instructions of Christ and His ascension into heaven. Luke will then begin the next of his two-part work by recapitulating and expanding upon this incident.

1. In the first lesson and the Gospel lesson, what were Jesus' last instructions to His disciples before He ascended into heaven? See Acts 1:4 and Luke 24:49. Had Jesus also given them any other instructions? For help see Matthew 28:18–20.

2. Why was it imperative that the disciples wait for the promised Holy Spirit? Verse 6 of the first lesson provides a clue. What did the disciples apparently think would now happen? See also Luke 19:11. How did their expectation differ from what Jesus had planned?

3. What else would they need that the Holy Spirit would bring? For help see Acts 1:8 and Luke 24:49. Why was this gift of the Holy Spirit necessary if the disciples were to carry out Jesus' plan?

4. After Jesus ascended into heaven, two men appeared to the disciples. Who where these men? For help see Mark 16:5. What did they say? To what event where they referring. For help see Luke 21:27.

5. Jesus had earlier talked about His ascension. Describe what He said by looking up the following passages: John 14:1–3 and John 16:5–7.

6. In the second lesson St. Paul prays that the Ephesians might "know" certain things. There are four things mentioned in the text. What are they? How are these four things known? For help, see Isaiah 11:2, Isaiah 6:9–10, and 2 Corinthians 4:6. Why are these things important for believers? For help, see Colossians 1:11, Ephesians 6:10–11, Romans 5:2–5, and Philippians 3:10–11.

7. Paul says that God seated Christ "at His right hand." How does Paul go on to describe what this means? See also 1 Peter 3:22.

Connect

1. Imagine that you were one of Jesus' disciples. You have listened to His teaching for the last three years, saw His crucifixion, and were overjoyed at His resurrection. Then He commanded you to "go and make disciples of all nations." And after saying that, He was taken up. What would be going through your heart and mind? How might you begin making disciples of all nations? Would you feel up to the task?

2. What has your church done as it tries to "make disciples of all nations"? What additional things might it do? What challenges does your church face in implementing these ideas? Are you up to the task? What did Jesus do for the disciples to help them face this task? What does Jesus promise you?

3. Evidently the disciples were still confused about God's plan of salvation, thinking that Jesus was still going to establish a glorious earthly kingdom. Why were they so confused? How was their confusion finally taken away? What application is there from this incident for your congregation as it faces uncertainty concerning how best to spend its resources?

4. St. Paul prays that believers be filled with hope. Why is hope such an important element for healthy living? What message of hope do you find in Christ's ascension? What impact might this hope have upon you and your congregation from day to day?

Vision

To Do This Week

1. It is important to have a plan when striving to reach a goal. Remembering that Christ has made you His witness, what might you plan to say to people who do not know Him? On a piece of paper write a simple presentation of the Gospel in your own words.
2. Revelation 5 takes believers into heaven to see Christ's exaltation in glory. Read this chapter for your devotions this week. What do you learn about Christ's authority?
3. During your devotions, make a list of God's gracious promises that you know of or are able to find in Scripture. Keep this list with you to strengthen your hope, particularly during times of hardship or uncertainty.

Closing Worship

Sing together stanzas 1, 2, and 5 of "Forth in Your Name, O Lord, I Go."

> Forth in Your name, O Lord, I go
> My daily labor to pursue,
> You, only You, resolved to know
> In all I think or speak or do.
>
> The task Your wisdom has assigned,
> Oh, let me cheerfully fulfill;
> In all my works Your presence find
> And prove Your good and perfect will.
>
> For You I joyously employ
> Whatever You in grace have giv'n
> I run my course with even joy,
> I closely walk with You to heav'n.

Scripture Lessons for the Seventh Sunday of Easter

In preparation for the next session, read Acts 1:15–26, 1 John 4:13–21, and John 17:11–19.

Lesson 16

Seventh Sunday of Easter

Acts 1:15–26; 1 John 4:13–21; John 17:11–19

Focus

Theme: *The Alien Life*

Law/Gospel Focus

Do not conform to evil in the world. Rather, stand and fight against it and your enemy, the devil. God Himself grants you the victory in Christ and will protect you in the fight.

Objectives

By the grace of God in Christ we will

1. understand more clearly the threats we face because we are not "of the world";
2. affirm our weakness and inability apart from the grace of God in Christ to withstand evil;
3. recognize how Christ "sanctifies" us and protects us from harm and danger;
4. give thanks that Christ gives us His victory over evil.

Opening Worship

Leader: In the name of the Father and of the Son and of the Holy Spirit.

Participants: Amen!

Leader: The LORD is my light and my salvation—

Participants: Whom shall I fear?

Leader: The LORD is the stronghold of my life—

Participants: Of whom shall I be afraid?

Leader: When evil men advance against me to devour my flesh,

Participants: When my enemies and my foes attack me, they will stumble and fall.

Introduction

The *Joy Luck Club* is a movie about cultural and generational crises. It is a story of Chinese immigrants, mothers anxious to preserve their ethnic identity and heritage, and daughters who struggle with their mothers' expectations as they blend into a foreign country. People who emigrate to another country often feel ill at ease, out of place, even threatened. The alien life is a difficult life.

1. If you have ever traveled to a foreign country, explain a little about the experience to the group. Were you ever nervous? Did you ever feel ill at ease? Why?

2. How do immigrants attempt to preserve their cultural identity?

3. Christians also are aliens. They are "in the world but not of the world." What is meant by this statement?

In the lessons today we will see how believers, because they belong to Christ, no longer belong to this world. We will learn more of what Jesus meant by this statement, what dangers we therefore face in the "foreign" land, and how God in Christ preserves us for our homeland in heaven.

Inform

Look at the summaries of the Scripture lessons for the Seventh Sunday of Easter. Then answer the questions.

Acts 1:15–26—Peter leads the believers in selecting a replacement for Judas, who had committed suicide after he betrayed Jesus.

1 John 4:13–21—John states that those who believe in Christ remain in Christ and are given His love, which frees them from fear and is demonstrated to others.

John 17:11–19—Jesus prays for the Father to protect His disciples while they remain in the world.

1. In the first lesson, Peter states that Scripture had to be fulfilled in regard to Judas. Peter then quotes two psalms. Locate these psalms. Who wrote them? To whom do these verses refer in the psalms? In what sense can they be applied to Judas?

2. Jesus also referred to Judas in the Gospel lesson. What did He say about him? Some might think on the basis of these passages that God himself had predestined Judas to eternal damnation. How would you respond to that idea? For help, see also John 3:16, 1 John 2:2, and Matthew 23:37. How then should we interpret what happened to Judas?

3. In the second lesson John describes what effect God's love has in a believer's life. What does he say in verse 16? In verse 18? In verses 20 and 21?

4. Many people say they love others. But love is subject to a variety of interpretations. Sometimes the word describes an emotion; at other times it describes an attitude, and still at other times a commitment. What does John mean when talks about God's love? For help, see Matthew 18:21–22, Matthew 5:38–42, John 14:15, and Matthew 5:43–48.

5. In the Gospel lesson Jesus asks the Father to protect His believers. From what do believers need protection? See verse 15 and also John 15:18–19, Matthew 24:9–10, and Ephesians 6:12. But also see Galatians 5:16–17.

6. How does Jesus ask the father to protect His followers? See verse 11 and verse 17. For help, look also at Romans 10:9–13 and Hebrews 4:12.

=========== **Connect** ===========

1. The lessons make clear that believers are aliens in the world. What points of comparison exist between a person's life in a foreign country and a believer's life on earth? Make a list of items.

2. When God created the world, He said it was good. There are in fact many blessings in this world, given for the enjoyment of all people. But because of sin, the world is also a hostile environment for believers. Their faith comes under direct and indirect attack.
a. Satan and evil angels are actively fighting against believers. In what form do they attack God's people?

b. Unbelievers and wicked people also attack the faith of God's people. In what way do they threaten the faith of God's people?

c. Believers, however, cannot always blame others for their own temptations. What does Galatians 5 tell us about threats to a believer's faith?

3. Jesus asked the father to "sanctify" His followers in truth. What does He mean by "sanctify," and how does He accomplish this in His Word? What does this have to do with a believer's preservation in the world?

4. Write a paragraph explaining what it means to be in the world but not of the world. Read your paragraph to the group.

5. Put yourself in the following situation. You have a friend by the

name of Bill, whom you have known for several years. He is not a believer, but he is an intelligent, kind, and helpful person at work and fun to be around. He has just turned 30 and wants you to go along with him and some other friends to Las Vegas for a night on the town. None of these other friends are believers either. Would you go along with them or not? Explain. How does the paragraph you wrote above enlighten your decision?

Vision

To Do This Week

1. Work with an immigrant or refugee. What might you do so that this person will feel more welcome, not only in this country, but also in the family of God?

2. Immigrants and refugees often dress and decorate their homes in distinctive ways to remind themselves of their homeland and to help preserve their own identity. This week consider what decoration or apparel you might employ as a constant reminder for yourself and others of your heavenly home.

Closing Worship

Sing stanzas 1, 2, and 4 of "God of Grace and God of Glory."
　　　God of grace and God of glory,
　　　On Your people pour Your pow'r;
　　　Crown Your ancient church's story;
　　　Bring its bud to glorious flow'r
　　　Grant us wisdom, grant us courage,
　　　For the facing of this hour,
　　　For the facing of this hour.

　　　Lo, the hosts of evil round us
　　　Scorn the Christ, assail His ways!
　　　From the fears that long have bound us
　　　Free our hearts to faith and praise.

Grant us wisdom, grant us courage
For the living of these days,
For the living of these days.

Save us from weak resignation
To the evils we deplore;
Let the gift of Your salvation
Be our glory evermore.
Grant wisdom, grant us courage,
Serving You whom we adore,
Serving You whom we adore.

Scripture Lessons for Pentecost

In preparation for the next session, read Ezekiel 37:1–14, Acts 2:22–36, and John 7:37–39.

Session 17

The Day of Pentecost

Ezekiel 37:1–14; Acts 2:22–36; John 7:37–39

Focus

Theme: *The Re-creation of Dead People*

Law/Gospel Focus

Because of their sinful rebellion against God, people are dead before God and without any lasting hope. God re-creates dead people through Christ, who sends His life-giving Spirit into the hearts of His people.

Objectives

By the grace of God in Christ we will
1. affirm how we are dead in sin before God;
2. describe the connection between Christ, the Holy Spirit, and new life;
3. affirm that God gives us life and hope in Christ through the Holy Spirit.

Opening Worship

Leader: In the name of the Father and of the Son and of the Holy Spirit.
Participants: Amen!
Leader: How many are Your works, O LORD!
Participants: In wisdom You made them all; the earth is full of Your creatures.
Leader: There is the sea, vast and spacious, teeming with creatures beyond number—
Participants: Living things both large and small.
Leader: There the ships go to and fro,
Participants: And the leviathan, which You formed to frolic there.

> Leader: These all look to You
> Participants: To give them their food at the proper time.
> Leader: When You give it to them,
> Participants: They gather it up;
> Leader: When You open Your hand,
> Participants: They are satisfied with good things.
> Leader: When You hide Your face,
> Participants: They are terrified;
> Leader: When You take away their breath,
> Participants: They die and return to dust.
> Leader: When You send Your Spirit,
> Participants: They are created, and You renew the face of the earth.
> (Psalm 104:24–30)

Introduction

Many churches find themselves facing new and increasingly difficult challenges. Some struggle to keep up with ethnographic changes within the community. Others desire to make the songs and words of worship more "dynamic" or "relevant" so that it will become more meaningful to those in attendance. Budgets often increase out of all proportion to available funds.

1. What are some challenges to ministry in your area?

2. What can your congregation do or has your congregation done to meet these challenges?

Today is known as the Day of Pentecost, an ancient feast day among the people of God. The day actually originated among the people of God in the Old Testament as a time for giving thanks for the harvest. But it is now celebrated by Christians in remembrance of the

Holy Spirit's coming in power. In the lessons for today we will meet individuals challenged by circumstance and learn how God graciously gives life and power through the Holy Spirit to meet the challenges they faced and the challenges faced by people today.

Inform

Look at the summaries of the Scripture lessons for the Day of Pentecost. Then answer the questions.

Ezekiel 37:1–14—Ezekiel sees a vision of dry bones, which are brought to life at the command of and by the Spirit of God.

Acts 2:22–36—Peter, filled with the Holy Spirit, addresses people on the Day of Pentecost, showing how the Scriptures had foretold the resurrection and exaltation of Jesus Christ.

John 7:37–39—On the last day of the Feast of Tabernacles, Jesus invites all to partake of the waters of life—the Holy Spirit.

1. Describe in your own words what Ezekiel saw and was commanded to do. This was not the first time when the "breath of God" gave life. What similarities are there between what you read in Genesis 2:7 and Ezekiel's vision?

2. What had happened to the Israelites so that they would describe themselves in such hopeless terms? What message of hope does the Lord speak by means of the vision? See verses 12–14.

3. How does Peter in the second lesson show from Scripture that Christ's resurrection and exaltation were foretold by God long ago among God's people? What Scriptures does he quote? How does he explain their application to Christ?

4. Peter shows by his words some rather penetrating insights into God's plan of salvation as foretold in Scripture. Had he always had such insight? For help see Acts 1:6. What had happened to Peter to explain the difference? For help, see Acts 1:8, John 16:13, and Luke 24:45–49. How did people react to Peter's sermon? For help see Acts 2:41.

5. In the Gospel lesson John tells how Jesus proclaimed these words on the "greatest day of the feast." This was the Feast of Tabernacles (John 7:2). It commemorated the time when Israel lived in tents in the wilderness and received from the Lord provisions for all its needs. For seven days water was taken from the pool of Siloam and carried in procession to the temple in remembrance of how God had provided water from the rock in the wilderness. The feast would conclude on the eighth day with a "holy assembly" that commemorated Israel's entrance into the Promised Land, "a land of springs of water." It was probably on this "greatest day of the feast," when no water was drawn, that Jesus proclaimed the words recorded in John. What connection is there between Jesus' words and this celebration?

Connect

1. Remember, we began this lesson by saying we would meet people who are challenged. In fact, each lesson shows us someone for whom God provides grace and power.
a. Who are the "challenged" people in the Old Testament lesson? What is the nature of their challenge? How does the Lord graciously respond to their challenge?

b. Who are the people challenged in the New Testament lesson? For help see Matthew 28:19–20. How did God graciously respond to their challenge?

c. Who are the people challenged in the Gospel lesson? How does Jesus graciously respond to their challenge?

2. What does the Holy Spirit do to and for the people of God? Look up the following passages.
1 Corinthians 12:3

Romans 15:13

Galatians 5:22–23

1 Corinthians 12:4–7

John 16:13

3. In the three lessons God brings hope to challenged people through the Holy Spirit. What connection is there between those people and your congregation?
a. What does God, the Holy Spirit, do for believers to restore their hope?

b. Like the disciples, congregations have been given a commission to make disciples of all peoples. What particular challenges does your congregation face in carrying out this commission? What does God, the Holy Spirit, do to help you meet them?

c. What hardships and dangers do individuals as yourself face from day to day? What does the Holy Spirit do for you to enable you to face such challenges?

Vision

To Do This Week

1. For your devotions, read through the book of Acts, keeping a list of all those things which the Holy Spirit does in the book. As you look through the list, think of how the Holy Spirit also works in your life.
2. The Holy Spirit brings gifts to the people of God. Read 1 Corinthians 12, Romans 12, and Ephesians 4. What gifts are mentioned in these Scripture references? Why are these gifts given? Think and pray about how the Holy Spirit will and does empower you for ministry in your congregation.

Closing Worship

Sing stanzas 1–3 of "Come, Holy Ghost, Our Souls Inspire."
    Come, Holy Ghost, our souls inspire,
    Ignite them with celestial fire;
    Spirit of God, You have the art
    Your gifts, the sev'nfold, to impart.

    Your blest outpouring from above
    Is comfort, life, and fire of love.
    Illumine with perpetual light
    The dullness of our blinded sight.

Anoint and cheer our much-soiled face
With the abundance of Your grace.
Keep far our foes; give peace at home;
Where You guide us, no ill can come.

Scripture Lessons for the Holy Trinity

In preparation for the next session, read Deuteronomy 6:4–9, Romans 8:14–17, and John 3:1–17.